MARTIAL ARTS SERIES

Taekwondo
Techniques & Tactics

Yeon Hwan Park
Secretary-General, United States Taekwondo Union
8th-Dan Black Belt

Tom Seabourne, PhD
Northeast Texas Community College
3rd-Dan Black Belt

Human Kinetics

C+

Library of Congress Cataloging-in-Publication Data

Park, Yeon Hwan
 Taekwondo techniques & tactics / Yeon Hwan Park, Tom Seabourne.
  p. cm. -- (Martial arts series)
  Includes bibliographical references and index.
  ISBN 0-88011-644-7
  1. Tae kwon do. 2. Tae kwon do—Training. I. Seabourne, Thomas. II. Title. III. Title:
Taekwondo techniques and tactics. IV. Series.
GV1114.9.P36 1997
796.8'153--DC21   96-37724
                                                                                                 CIP

ISBN: 0-88011-644-7

Acquisitions Editor: Kenneth Mange; **Developmental Editor:** Julie A. Marx; **Assistant Editors:**
Andrew Smith, Julia Anderson, and Sandra Merz Bott; **Editorial Assistant:** Jennifer Hemphill;
Copyeditor: Holly Gilly; **Proofreader:** Julia Anderson; **Indexer:** Theresa Schaefer; **Graphic De-
signer:** Robert Reuther; **Graphic Artists:** Sandra Meier and Tom Roberts; **Photo Editor:** Boyd
LaFoon; **Cover Designer:** Jack Davis; **Cover Photographer:** Ray Malace; **Interior Photographers:**
Ron Barker and Dave Scudder; **Illustrators:** Keith Blomberg and Terry Hayden; **Printer:** United
Graphics

Human Kinetics books are available at special discounts for bulk purchase. Special editions or book
excerpts can also be created to specification. For details, contact the Special Sales Manager at Human
Kinetics.

Printed in the United States of America   10   9   8   7   6   5   4   3   2   1

Human Kinetics
Web site: http://www.humankinetics.com/

United States: Human Kinetics, P.O. Box 5076, Champaign, IL 61825-5076
1-800-747-4457
e-mail: humank@hkusa.com

Canada: Human Kinetics, Box 24040, Windsor, ON N8Y 4Y9
1-800-465-7301 (in Canada only)
e-mail: humank@hkcanada.com

Europe: Human Kinetics, P.O. Box IW14, Leeds LS16 6TR, United Kingdom
(44) 1132 781708
e-mail: humank@hkeurope.com

Australia: Human Kinetics, 57A Price Avenue, Lower Mitcham, South Australia 5062
(08) 277 1555
e-mail: humank@hkaustralia.com

New Zealand: Human Kinetics, P.O. Box 105-231, Auckland 1
(09) 523 3462
e-mail: humank@hknewz.com

I DEDICATE THIS BOOK TO ALL OF THE PEOPLE, YOUNG AND OLD, WHO HAVE BEEN AND WILL CONTINUE TO BE TOUCHED BY THIS OMNIPOTENT ART, TAEKWONDO. IT HAS GIVEN ME SO MUCH BENEFIT THROUGHOUT MY LIFE, AND I HOPE THAT MANY MORE WILL HAVE THE OPPORTUNITY TO REAP ITS REWARDS.

—YEON HWAN PARK

I DEDICATE THIS BOOK TO MEMBERS OF THE MEN'S AND WOMEN'S UNITED STATES OLYMPIC TAEKWONDO MOVEMENT— PAST, PRESENT, AND FUTURE.

—TOM SEABOURNE

CONTENTS

PREFACE

aekwondo has been around for centuries and has a strong international following. It is incredibly good for you because it affects every aspect of your being. People practice taekwondo as an Olympic sport, an art, or a lifestyle. Taekwondo is all-encompassing. It incorporates relaxation and motivational techniques, stretching, strengthening, jumping, kicking, and striking. Practicing taekwondo improves your flexibility, body alignment, concentration, confidence, balance, strength, speed, endurance, and your ability to defend yourself—all while decreasing body fat and stress levels. Most practitioners sleep well, are in good physical condition, have lean bodies, and follow a disciplined lifestyle. Taekwondo becomes that magic place where peak experiences occur.

Although taekwondo has a strong following, it needs to be demystified. Taekwondo *is* punching and kicking, but it is more than just that physical expression. With as little as two hours of practice each week, you can use taekwondo to relieve stress and improve your ability to defend yourself. You can burn excess calories, have fun, break your normal routine, and forget about time. In addition, taekwondo is good for children. It teaches them about respect, self-confidence, and discipline. Taekwondo encourages you to try your best, but with patience. You learn to accept your limitations without having them hold you back. The traditions and customs of taekwondo are your framework for control and discipline. Training, like virtue, is its own reward.

This book will benefit anyone who wants to learn more about taekwondo, from its history and rules to the basic techniques. The first three chapters of *Taekwondo Techniques & Tactics* give you an overview of the art of taekwondo, including tips on choosing a taekwondo school, a short history of the roots and current status of taekwondo, and a list of Korean terms often heard in the training hall. Chapters 4 through 9 are filled with illustrated, step-by-step procedures for a variety of falls, rolls, stances, arm strikes, kicks, blocks, and steps. Chapter 10 includes information on the forms practice that is an integral part of taekwondo training and competition. Chapter 11 gives you suggestions for preparing your personal strategy using your strengths and a variety of combinations and counterattacks. Chapter 12 gives an overview of taekwondo competition and provides information about preparing both mentally and physically to compete. Finally, chapter 13 illustrates solid cardiovascular, flexibility, resistance, and plyometric exercises to improve your taekwondo performance.

No matter your age or experience, *Taekwondo Techniques & Tactics* is a valuable tool. You can adjust the parameters of training to fit your lifestyle, whether you are interested in competition, fitness, or self-defense. For example, a mental toughness program may be beneficial if you are in a high-stress job; plyometrics and sparring may be helpful if you compete. You choose your method of preparation for each situation. *Taekwondo Techniques & Tactics* teaches you to synthesize salient aspects of different disciplines to shape your own program. You design your personal and unique formula for optimal taekwondo performance. Target your strengths and weaknesses and individualize strategies to meet your needs. Use the techniques that work best for your body structure, your personality, and the demands of each situation. *Taekwondo Techniques & Tactics* helps you select what fits your physique. Practice kicks that are practical for your leg length, and tailor arm strikes to fit your upper-body strength. Depending on your personality, you may be a defensive fighter or a counterattacker, or you may decide simply to beat your opponent to the punch. In *Taekwondo Techniques & Tactics,* you use what works for you and discard the rest.

To begin, look closely at the photographs in the book and then copy them. View the entire movement without analysis. Select an exercise and begin the step-by-step instruction. But rather than mindlessly practicing hundreds of different attacks, pick a movement and hone it into a personal weapon. Don't try to do too much too soon, though. It is better to practice for half an hour three times a week than to get burned out and quit after practicing two hours every day. The techniques take practice, but you can gain the rewards through hard work and without mysticism.

Don't just take our word about the benefits of taekwondo. Read through *Taekwondo Techniques & Tactics* and see for yourself. Start today. The sooner you start, the sooner you'll gain more personal satisfaction. In just over a month, your techniques will be sharp. In six months you will be confident. You'll be able to respond to situations rather than to blindly react to them. Most important, you'll start to develop the three traits successful taekwondoists possess: They master one, maybe two, techniques; they are mentally tough; and they are in great shape. We hope *Taekwondo Techniques & Tactics* helps you master new skills and achieve the balance of body and mind you are seeking.

ACKNOWLEDGMENTS

THANK YOU TO MY PARENTS, MY WIFE AND CHILDREN,
MY JUNIORS AND SENIORS, AND MY STUDENTS FOR THEIR
OVERWHELMING SUPPORT THROUGHOUT MY CAREER AS A
COMPETITOR, INSTRUCTOR, AND SUPPORTER OF TAEKWONDO.
I WOULD ALSO LIKE TO THANK THE UNITED STATES
TAEKWONDO UNION, THE WORLD TAEKWONDO FEDERATION,
AND MY BROTHER YEON HEE PARK,
FOR IT WAS MY DESIRE TO BE LIKE MY BROTHER
THAT FIRST INSPIRED ME TO STUDY TAEKWONDO.

—YEON HWAN PARK

THANKS TO MY PARENTS, ANN AND TOM; MY WIFE, DANESE; AND
MY CHILDREN, ALAINA, GRANT, LAURA, SUSANNA, AND JULIA
FOR ALLOWING ME TO TRAIN ENDLESS HOURS IN TAEKWONDO.
THANKS TO MY MASTER INSTRUCTOR, SOON HO CHANG, WHO
HELPED ME COMPETE AT MY POTENTIAL.
THANKS ALSO TO MY FRIENDS MILES HALL AND ERNEST
HERNDON, AND TO MY DEVELOPMENTAL EDITOR JULIE MARX AND
THE REST OF THE STAFF AT HUMAN KINETICS FOR HELPING
MAKE A DREAM COME TRUE.

—TOM SEABOURNE

CHAPTER

1

GETTING STARTED

Taekwondo, the Korean art of self-defense, is literally translated as "foot, hand, way." The simple translation says a lot more about the meaning of this ancient martial art than you might first suspect. First, the word *foot* suggests that the use of kicking techniques is an important part of taekwondo. In fact, leg techniques comprise about 70 percent of a taekwondo practitioner's arsenal. The word *hand* tells us that punches, chops, elbow strikes, and finger jabs make up the remaining 30 percent. The word "way," however, is not obvious.

The true power of the art of taekwondo is found in the simple two-letter word that means "way." The *do* in taekwondo implies not only a physical means by which the techniques are performed, but also the practitioner's mental and spiritual connection to the techniques. Although taekwondo is very much about kicking, punching, self-defense, board breaking, and competition, it greatly transcends these physical boundaries. It is a discipline of mind and body, a modern world sport, and a philosophy.

THE BENEFITS OF TAEKWONDO

Ask any white belt with two or three months of training what he has gained so far from his taekwondo experiences, and the answer may surprise you. Certainly he will talk about improved flexibility, strength, and overall fitness, but he is likely to conclude by pointing to improved self-respect and self-confidence. Through many long hours of arduous training and struggle to overcome fatigue and other physical limitations, the taekwondo practitioner perseveres to forge his will and enhance his life.

The taekwondo school (*dojang*) is a special place, a world unto itself. You take off your shoes before entering the dojang and bow when you step onto the practice floor. In the dojang, you are introduced to a code of ethics and morality that teachers nurture and strictly enforce. Respect, discipline, self-control, and honesty are more than words you hear—they are concepts you learn to live by. The new adult student will learn a lot about humility. Everyone comes to the school on the same level, regardless of race, religion, or economic or professional status. No one is given special consideration, and everyone is judged on diligent practice and dedication to the school, the art, and each other.

The sense of values and the discipline learned from taekwondo are big reasons for its popularity. Even very young children benefit from taekwondo training. A few may go on to become tournament champions, but all can develop a sense of discipline at an early age. Discipline sets taekwondo apart from many other sports. Children may laugh when a playmate misses a kickball, but comrades in taekwondo will help a fallen opponent to his feet. Today's taekwondo champions learned discipline early. Their physical, mental, and moral character development led them to avoid tobacco, alcohol, and other drugs. These athletes developed their bodies into extraordinary fighting machines. Through belt progression, tournaments, and arduous training, they earned recognition from their peers. They say "yes, sir" and "no, sir" and refer to their instructors as "Mr." or "Ms." Punches and kicks are only half of the training; the other half is discipline and focus.

Choosing a School

Look under Martial Arts in your local yellow pages and you'll be treated to a smorgasbord of martial arts advertisements: kung fu, karate, jujitsu, hapkido, aikido, and various organizations such as the United States Taekwondo Union (USTU), the American Taekwondo Association (ATA), and the United States Taekwondo Federation (USTF). Choosing an art demands very serious consideration, because the style you choose to study will be a long-term commitment. Visit a number of martial arts schools and watch classes to see which style of martial arts appeals to you and to be aware of what style the school teaches. Many schools teach a modern blend of many arts instead of the traditional arts. As you make your decision to train in the martial arts, be aware of your own body makeup and limitations. Not all arts are appealing to all people, so it's a good idea to take a trial lesson or two before making a long-term commitment.

Martial Arts Styles

Most martial arts can be characterized as hard or soft and as linear or circular. Taekwondo is generally considered a hard, or external, style, which means its techniques consist of strikes, kicks, and blocks. Taekwondo practitioners strike their opponents with the hard surfaces of their body, such as the fist or the heel of the foot. In comparison, aikido is a soft, or internal, style. Aikido practitioners do not generally strike their opponents, but rather parry and sidestep the attack, using the attackers' force against them rather than meeting the force head on.

Taekwondo is also linear. The shortest distance between two points is a straight line. Taekwondo depends on short, quick, powerful strikes, such as the reverse punch or side kick. Aikido, on the other hand, is circular, involving a lot of footwork to avoid an attack. Shotokan karate, Muay Thai kickboxing, and Kenpo karate are also hard, linear styles similar to taekwondo. Jujitsu, tai chi chuan, and hapkido are soft, circular styles. Some styles like Wing Chun and Okinawan gojuryu combine equal elements of hard/soft and linear/circular.

A student training in the arts needs to set specific goals. Do you wish to compete? Are you strictly interested in self-defense? Are you interested in an art with a rich history and deep philosophy? Would you like to memorize forms? Do you wish to study a flashy and acrobatic style of martial arts? For example, Shotokan karate and some styles of kung fu require students to learn many forms. Muay Thai kickboxing, on the other hand, has no forms but is very physically demanding. Aikido is a highly philosophical and beautiful art, but its practitioners don't compete. Jujitsu is a self-defense art, but it does not emphasize high, flashy kicks. However, the student of taekwondo is fortunate to have the opportunity to learn forms (*poomse*, or a series of movements against imaginary opponents), compete in tournaments, study practical self-defense, learn about history and philosophy, and do an occasional flashy kick.

SELECTING A TAEKWONDO SCHOOL

When you have selected a martial art and are ready to pick your school, phone several studios and ask if you can observe a class. Make an appointment to watch a class and imagine yourself as a

student. Pay attention to the level of discipline in the class and watch the other students. Do they seem to be catching on? If you are most interested in self-defense and fitness, a school that focuses solely on competition might not be the best choice for you. Conversely, if you are interested in competition, choose a school where you'll have the opportunity to compete. A certified USTU school is the only taekwondo organization under the auspices of the World Taekwondo Federation (WTF). Therefore, if your goal is to have a chance to compete in the Olympics or other international tournaments, enroll in a USTU school.

Here are some key qualities to look for when choosing a taekwondo school:

- The head instructor is friendly, personable, and accessible.
- The head instructor is a certified sabumnim (master) with the WTF.
- All assistants are certified by the WTF and have cardio-pulmonary resuscitation (CPR) certification.
- Classes are structured and organized well.
- Separate classes are held for children and adults, and beginners have their own classes.
- The school is clean, well staffed, and run professionally.
- Prospective students are allowed to observe class.
- If the school uses contracts or outside billing agencies, all conditions are clearly spelled out in writing.

In general, go with your instincts. The school should have a good reputation and a good balance of family atmosphere and discipline.

After visiting several studios, choose one that allows you to pay monthly and gives you the most class time for your money. Huge studios with extensive workout facilities are common in some large cities. Showers, locker rooms, and exercise facilities are nice amenities, but the most important thing is quality of instruction.

Try a school for three months. In that time, you should learn all of the basic punches, kicks, strikes, and blocks and feel confident in your ability to handle yourself. With a few more years of training, you should develop a general mastery of basic techniques and integrate an understanding of the philosophy and principles of taekwondo. In most schools, this level of knowledge is signified with the award of black belt. (If you would like more information about taekwondo schools in your area contact The United States Taekwondo Union, One Olympic Plaza, Suite 405, Colorado Springs, CO 80909, 719-578-4632.)

TAEKWONDO CLASS

The typical taekwondo class will differ from school to school, but most follow the pattern of the sixty-minute class described here.

Before class, students are expected to warm up quietly without supervision. A loud clap of the instructor's hands signals that class will begin. Students line up according to rank. Advanced students move to the front of the group, with the higher belts on the right. Experienced students with higher belts are expected to be good role models both inside and outside of the dojang. They set an example for their classmates. Each class session begins with a ceremonial bow initiated by the instructor. Some taekwondo schools recite a creed honoring their instructor, school, and country. After this show of respect, the students practice warm-up and stretching routines, like the ones you'll find in chapter 13. The warm-up time is followed by about 15 minutes of basic arm strikes, kicks, and blocking drills. You'll spend another 15 minutes performing stepping exercises, combinations, and counterattacks. The final 30 minutes is devoted to sparring and poomse. Class ends with a bow.

The taekwondo school is a unique place, but don't confine your practice just to the dojang. You can practice vigorous, disciplined taekwondo anytime, anywhere. You can surreptitiously focus on a taekwondo breathing technique or, with as little as six square feet, you can punch, kick, block, strike, and practice your forms. As a youngster, Tom Seabourne was eager to master his art and shadow sparred in hotel rooms and airports, practiced kicks in bus stations, target trained on tennis courts, and practiced forms in racquetball courts.

Ⓒommon Rules of the Training Hall

- Keep talking at a minimum during rest periods; don't talk at all while class is in session.
- Use the minutes before practice begins and during breaks in the class to work on your taekwondo.
- Show respect at all times for your instructor and fellow students.
- Outside of class, practice your taekwondo skills in unprovocative settings. Fighting outside of the dojang may be grounds for your dismissal, unless you are fighting for your life in a self-defense situation.
- Loose-fitting clothing, shorts, a warm-up suit, or a taekwondo uniform is acceptable attire for training.
- When you purchase a taekwondo uniform, ask your instructor to demonstrate how to tie the belt.
- Remove all jewelry before you begin training, and be sure that your fingernails and toenails do not have any sharp edges.
- Don't chew gum during practice.
- Remove eyeglasses and contact lenses before participating in any type of sparring activities, unless you wear eye guards. Wear a mouth guard and a protective cup (for men) when sparring.
- When you practice with a partner, strike with accuracy and control. Good sporting behavior and courtesy are essential during sparring.
- Never criticize other martial arts styles or instructors.

Belts and Ranks

Taekwondo awards six different colors of belts. You advance by participating in classes; learning and performing basic techniques, combinations, and poomse; and sparring. Each student begins as a white belt and, after learning prerequisite skills, takes tests to advance through yellow, green, blue, red, and, after several years of training, black (see tables 1.1 and 1.2). Belt tests and belt rank are uniform among USTU sanctioned schools. However, a red belt in a USTU system may be equivalent to a black belt in another style of taekwondo. Children may test alongside adults until testing for black belt. Red belt students

TABLE 1.1
Sample Student Belt Progression*

Class (Gup)	Belt	Cumulative training time
10th	White	Beginner
8th	Yellow	3 months
6th	Green	6 months
4th	Blue	9 months
2nd	Red	1 year
1st	Red	2 years
(Next level is 1st-degree black belt)		

*9th, 7th, 5th, and 3rd Gup in this sample system are levels within the white, yellow, green, and blue belts, respectively.

TABLE 1.2
Sample Instructor Belt Progression

Degree (Dan)	Name	Cumulative training time
1st	Cho Dan	3 years
2nd	Yi-dan	5 years
3rd	Sam-dan	7 years
4th	Sa-dan	9 years
5th	Oh-dan	11 years
6th	Yook Dan	15 years
7th*	Chil Dan	20 or more years
8th	Pal Dan	20 or more years
9th	Koo Dan	20 or more years
10th	Sip Dan	20 or more years

*7th degree and above must demonstrate significant contribution to the art and sport of taekwondo.

under 13 years may test and receive a junior black belt. Junior black belts may compete in junior tournaments at the state, national, and international levels. After age 18, students automatically qualify for the senior division and may compete in open USTU tournaments. White belt students may compete in tournaments with their instructor's permission after they have been training for a minimum of three months. Belts below black are referred to as *Gup,* or class, and start from tenth Gup to first Gup (the rank just prior to black belt). First Gup students working toward their black belts teach classes, under their instructor's supervision. By the time they reach black belt, most participants have had more than 60 hours of teaching experience. Black belt begin with first degree ranks (Dan) and promotions lead to tenth degree. Taekwondo black belts understand that achieving their first Dan symbolizes the beginning of their training.

Taekwondo is an art, a sport, and a way of life. Each day of training brings you closer to perfection. For example, through the course of your training, you will practice your front kick thousands of times. As a white belt, you are satisfied simply to maintain your balance throughout a kick. When you attain your blue belt, you will throw a front kick accurately to chest level. As a black belt, you will throw a powerful and controlled front kick with either leg to any area of your opponent's body.

Taekwondo is not just physical. Control separates training in a dojang from fighting in a street brawl. Taekwondo students learn to throw strikes, punches, and kicks with lethal speed and force for self-defense, yet they can control their movements to snap a powerful kick inches from their training partner. Students of all ages learn a discipline of mind and body they carry through life.

CHAPTER

2

ROOTS
OF TAEKWONDO

Most people today are familiar with the martial arts, but do you know how they were created? It is fascinating to think back to their beginnings 5,000 years ago when martial training systematized punches, kicks, strikes, and blocks into an art form. Traditions and styles of practice have changed through the years, and all add to the enjoyment of practicing taekwondo today.

THE BEGINNING OF MARTIAL ARTS

There is evidence that empty-handed fighting techniques existed in India, Egypt, and China 5,000 years ago. Legend suggests Bodhidharma, a Buddhist monk, traveled from India to China and taught Buddhism to Chinese monks at a Shaolin temple during the sixth century A.D. Meditation, yoga, and martial arts were his messages. The Chinese named Bodhidharma's discipline *kung fu*.

Buddhist monks and Zen masters continued to pass down combat strategies from generation to generation. Soon these holy men began teaching others, and the arts proliferated throughout the East.

Martial arts entered Korea more than 4,000 years ago, during the Koguryo, Paekche, and Silla dynasties. Archaeological findings of sculptures and murals suggest that the people in these three kingdoms practiced defensive postures (*tae kyon*) resembling the traditional sparring stances of today. King Jin Heung of the Silla dynasty, which lasted from 668 to 918 A.D., developed the *Hwarang-do* ("the way of flowering manhood") society. The society followed a fundamental education and fitness program that first taught the elements of tae kyon at a military academy for young nobility. The tenets of Hwarang-do were obedience and respect to parents and loyalty to the nation. Along with martial arts training, the Hwarang-do followed a code emphasizing honor, courage, faithfulness, and peace. The tremendous spiritual influence of the Hwarang-do was responsible for the unification of the Koguryo, Paekche, and Silla dynasties and the spread of tae kyon throughout Korea.

THE DEVELOPMENT OF TAEKWONDO

During the Koryo dynasty (918-1392), tae kyon became known as *subak*, and the focus of martial arts changed from a fitness and recreational system to a military fighting art. Subak was divided into several systems and was practiced by the military as well as the general public. Disciples spread the art by holding demonstrations and competitions. In 1790, during the Yi dynasty (1392-1910), Lee Duk Mu wrote *Muye Dobo Tongji*, the first Korean martial arts textbook with an entire chapter devoted to taekwondo. This book served to popularize the art among the general public, which contributed to its survival in a time when changing political views made military activities unpopular. However, during the second half of the Yi dynasty, subak practice declined, until the limited knowledge was being passed on only in fragments from generation to generation in individual families.

Japan invaded Korea in 1909 and banned the practice of all Korean martial arts. However, the ban sparked a renewed interest

The Kukkiwon.

in subak, and many people studied the art secretly under famous masters. Others left Korea to study martial arts in Japan or China. Secretive practice ended and interest in the martial arts continued to grow when judo, karate, and kung fu were introduced to Korea in 1943. When Japan freed Korea in 1945, Korea's own martial arts had a chance to grow. Many different schools (*kwans*) of Korean martial arts existed for several years, each one focusing on a different style of tae kyon/subak, including soo bahk do, kwon bop, and tang soo do. Tae kyon became a regular part of Korean military training in the 10 years following Korea's freedom from Japanese rule, but disagreements between the kwans kept a unified national organization from being developed. Finally, in 1955, a meeting was held to unify the various kwans, and taekwondo was chosen in 1957 as the official name for Korean martial arts. The Korean Taekwondo Association was formed in 1961, and thousands of taekwondo demonstrations held throughout the world during the 1960s served to firmly establish worldwide interest in this Korean martial art.

In 1972, an exquisite gymnasium called the Kukkiwon was designed and built in Seoul, Korea, specifically for the education and training of Korean taekwondo students. One year later, the Kukkiwon hosted the first world taekwondo championships with 200 competitors from 17 countries. The Kukkiwon has remained the headquarters for modern elementary, high school, collegiate, and Olympic taekwondo associations throughout the world. The World Taekwondo Federation was also created in 1973. Since its inception, the WTF has been the only regulating body for taekwondo that is recognized by the Korean government.

In 1974, taekwondo was accepted into the Amateur Athletic Union (AAU) of the United States. AAU taekwondo was presided over by Un Yong Kim following the precepts of the WTF. In 1981, the organization's name was changed from the AAU Taekwondo Union to the United States Taekwondo Union (USTU). And in 1984, the USTU was approved as a "Group A" member of the United States Olympic Committee, under the umbrella of the WTF.

In 1988, taekwondo made its first appearance in the Olympic Games as an exhibition sport in Seoul, Korea. Taekwondo remained a demonstration sport in the 1992 Games in Barcelona, Spain, and will be an official medal sport in the 2000 Games in Sydney, Australia. Since 1988 taekwondo has flourished, and it is practiced by more than 20 million people in 112 countries. Male and female students of all ages compete using rules similar to those practiced 2,000 years ago. Competition begins at the state level and progresses to national and international status. International events include the Junior Olympics, Collegiate Championships, World Games, World Cup, World Championships, Pan American Games, and the Olympic Games.

TAEKWONDO TODAY

Modern taekwondo retains much of its original artistry and tradition. Traditional postures have been passed down through the generations. The sport of taekwondo has changed dramatically, however. Protective equipment, electronic scoring, biomechanical analysis, and videotaping have made taekwondo a standout among the martial arts. Although grappling sports, such as wrestling and judo, have been part of the Olympic Games for years, taekwondo is the only nongloved martial art to be accepted as an Olympic sport. Japanese karate, Chinese kung fu, and a variety of other self-defense disciplines share similar punches, kicks, strikes, and blocks with taekwondo, but these other styles fail to enjoy taekwondo's worldwide organization and representation.

3

LANGUAGE
OF TAEKWONDO

Korea was the birthplace of taekwondo. Unfortunately, taekwondoists from other countries may not be privy to the principles and standards of the Korean culture. Therefore, beginning students have the responsibility to develop an understanding of Korean customs and language.

Relationships are very important in Korea. The need for strict order and decorum is obvious when you understand the overcrowded conditions. Korea had an average of 828 people per square mile in 1994, making it one of the most densely populated countries of the world. Basic rules allow Korean society to function. Everyone understands his or her place in the social hierarchy. One's social position depends on age and education. An older, more experienced individual is referred to as a *senior,* and seniors are always respected and honored.

Politeness and discipline are exported from Korean society to the American dojang in several ways. For example, a simple bow from the waist is a traditional greeting of respect. Senior (advanced) students position themselves at the head of the class, and subordinates follow seniors at the drinking fountain and in eating establishments. In addition, sitting with the legs crossed, smoking, or wearing sunglasses in the presence of a senior is discourteous.

The heritage of taekwondo is further rooted in the Korean language. The Korean language is tough to learn because, in addition to its own characteristics, it incorporates Chinese elements. The more fluent speakers become, the more they use the Chinese dialect in their speech. The Korean alphabet has 10 vowels and 14 consonants, but Chinese characters must be learned also.

In most dojangs you will hear an instructor barking Korean commands. Taekwondo tournament players are required to understand Korean terminology. It is not unusual to observe more than 60 countries competing in international taekwondo events without miscommunication.

TRAINING TERMS

The following list contains some of the most common Korean terms you will encounter in your training. To help you learn the basics of the Korean language, here are some simple pronunciation rules:

- The letter *a* is a pronounced with a short vowel sound, such as in *fawn*.
- When you see *wa*, imagine adding an *h* to sound like *hwa*.
- *Yu* sounds like *you*.
- *Ya* rhymes with *pa*.
- *Ae* is a long *a*, as in *pay*.
- The letter *e* is short, like in *red*.
- The letter *i* is short, like in *it*.
- The letter *o* is long, like in *so*.

cha-gi—Kick. Kicks are used in taekwondo both for self-defense and competition. Taekwondo enthusiasts are known for their versatile and powerful kicking technique. No other martial art places as much emphasis on kicking as taekwondo does. Cha-gi also refers to the striking surfaces of the foot used to hit a vital area.

KICKS	
Korean	**English**
ahp cha-gi	front kick
ahn bandul cha-gi	crescent kick (out to in)
backat bandul cha-gi	crescent kick (in to out)
dolryo cha-gi	roundhouse kick
dwi cha-gi	back kick
gullgi cha-gi	hook kick
nerya cha-gi	axe kick
twi o-cha-gi	jumping kick
yop cha-gi	side kick

STRIKING SURFACES—KICKS

Korean	English
ahp-chook	ball of foot
baaldung	instep
baalnul	knife foot (foot edge)
dwi-chook	heel

cha-ryot sogi—Attention stance. Although there are many stances in taekwondo, cha-ryot sogi is perhaps the most significant because everything starts from this position. Stand with both feet together, hands directly at your sides, and look straight ahead. While in this stance, you must stand perfectly still and concentrate on the instructor's directions. See *sogi* for a complete list of the stances included in this book.

chi-gi—Strikes and punches. Strikes and punches are quicker than kicks. They also allow for more stability. Chi-gi also refers to the striking surfaces of the arm and hand that are used to hit a vital area.

STRIKES AND PUNCHES

Korean	English
ahp chi-gi	front punch
ahp-joomock ji-roukee	jab
ahre chi-gi	low punch
bandae ji-roukee	reverse punch
ba-tang-son chi-gi	palm heel strike
dung-joomock chi-gi	back fist strike
gullgi chi-gi	hook punch
momtong chi-gi	center punch
palkoop chi-gi	elbow strike
son-nal chi-gi	knife hand strike
wee (eolgul) chi-gi	high (face) punch
yop chi-gi	side punch

STRIKING SURFACES—STRIKES AND PUNCHES

Korean	English
ba-tang-son	palm heel
joomock	fist
me-joomock	hammer fist
palkoop	elbow
pyon-joomock	open knuckle fist
son-kut	fingertips
son-nal	knife hand
son-nal dung	spear hand

dojang—Taekwondo school. A dojang is a highly treasured place to a taekwondo practitioner. It is treated with great respect and pride.

dobok/di—The white V-neck uniform a student wears to practice taekwondo. The di is the belt worn around the waist. All students must wear a clean dobok. The uniform is white as a symbol of purity and ignorance. In ancient times, people wore white belts to hold up their pants. As they trained, the belt became dirtier and the color darker. That's why, in modern taekwondo schools, you receive a progressively darker colored belt as you get promoted.

dong chak—Any specific movement in taekwondo. It may be a punch, kick, strike, block, or step. Perform each move with speed and power according to the guidelines of your instructor.

dorra—A command to reverse your direction. This command is usually given at the end of a set of stepping movements so that the students can turn and resume their steps in the opposite direction.

guk-gi—Flag. The Korean flag hangs beside a flag of the home country. When a student enters the dojang, he bows to the practice rooms and to both flags out of respect. The home country's flag hangs in the dojang to show respect and to honor it for the freedom to practice the art of taekwondo there. The Korean flag is in the dojang to show respect to the country of origin of the art of taekwondo. Very often at tournaments and other special events, both flags and countries are saluted with the singing of the national anthems.

Hwarang-do—Literal translation is "the way of flowering manhood." Hwarang refers to members of a royal family who lived in the Silla kingdom. Modern taekwondo traces its ethical and physical language from the ancient "Hwarang."

joonbi—The directive to assume the ready position. From the ready position you should be prepared to move in any direction, with any technique, according to the command of your instructor.

kibon—A basic technique, such as one that a beginner might learn in his first three months of training. Kibon may include basic kicks, punches, strikes, and blocks.

ki-hop—The loud, guttural yell often heard from taekwondo students during practice. It is important that this yell comes from the pit of your stomach. This will ensure that you are breathing from your diaphragm and not taking shallow breaths. The ki-hop will also give you more power, improve your confidence, and may even frighten your opponent.

kup so—A vital spot on the body vulnerable to attack.

Korean	English
balmock	ankle
eolgul	face
huri	waist
mok	neck
momtong	body
mo-li	head
moo-rup	knee
sonmock	wrist
tuk	chin

kwan—Style of taekwondo school. When Japan freed Korea in 1945, the art of taekwondo began to spread. However, there were many different styles of taekwondo. Some of the kwans were moo duk kwan, chung do kwan, and ji do kwan.

kwanchangnim—Grand master. Technically, this highly respected title is reserved for the head of a style or school of taekwondo; however, any instructor with the rank of seventh-degree black belt or higher is usually referred to as kwanchangnim out of respect for his years of dedication to the art. An instructor who has received this title is not only a highly skilled practitioner of taekwondo, but also contributes to and promotes the art.

kyorugi—Sparring. Kyorugi is generally the focal point of taekwondo competition. Taekwondo sparring is fast-paced and vigorous. Free sparring is one of the best ways for students to test their techniques and combinations. To be a good taekwondo sparring competitor, you need endurance, speed, balance, agility, focus, timing, and strategy. Sparring competition is usually categorized according to sex, age, weight, and rank.

kyukpah—Board breaking. The purpose of kyukpah in taekwondo is to test the students' focus and power and to help the students overcome their fear of striking the board. Kyukpah is not only an impressive demonstration of skill, but it also helps develop confidence.

kyong-ye—To bow. Bowing is a traditional way of showing respect. It doesn't imply subservience to anyone. We bow to show respect to our school, flag, art, instructors, and ourselves. It is imperative that we bow with sincerity. Be sure to bow slowly (take about four seconds), bending at the waist and looking down. By not looking at the person you bow to, you show respect and trust.

maggi—A block. Blocks are used to defend against an attack. Taekwondo blocks are hard blocks, executed with speed and power. A taekwondo block can be thrown with such force that it may break an attacker's arm or leg.

Korean	English
ahn maggi	middle inner block
ahre maggi	low (downward) block
backat maggi	middle outer block
momtong maggi	middle block
son-nal maggi	knife hand block
wee (eolgul) maggi	rising (face) block
yeot pero maggi	X-block

nak buhp—Falling. Nak buhp techniques are important to prevent injury. When you fall properly, you absorb the impact on a part of the body that is not easily injured. Learn how to roll and slap the ground to reduce the stress of the fall.

Korean	English
hoo bang nak buhp	fall or roll to the back
hwee jeon nak buhp	rolling (forward)
jeon bank nak buhp	fall to the front
jwa chook bang nak buhp	fall to the left side
woo chook bang nak buhp	fall to the right side

poomse—Forms. Poomse is the artistic side of taekwondo. All WTF (World Taekwondo Federation) schools practice the Tae Geuk series of forms. These prearranged movements combine blocks, punches, kicks, and stances in an attempt to develop balance, distance, power, and grace. A well-executed poomse uses a unified mind and body.

sabomnim—A taekwondo master. This title of respect is usually reserved for someone with a rank of at least a fifth-degree black belt. A sabomnim is not only a teacher, but also a friend who will guide your development with care and patience.

sho—A command to relax. This command is usually given at the conclusion of a set of exercises.

sogi—Stance. Taekwondo stances are low and provide a strong base of support. Taekwondo stances are the foundation for all blocks, kicks, and strikes.

Korean	English
ahp-gubi sogi	front stance
ahp sogi	walking stance
cha-ryot sogi	attention stance
dwi-gubi sogi	back stance
gyo-rugi sogi	fighting stance
juchoom sogi	horse stance
joonbi sogi	ready stance

COUNTING TERMS

Becoming familiar with Korean numbers will help you as you listen to your instructor count off the number of repetitions to perform or as you listen for your score during a competition. The numbers from 1 to 10 are hana, dul, set, net, dasot, yasot, elgub, yodol, ahob, yol.

Taekwondo is practiced by hundreds of countries throughout the world, but practitioners can communicate if they have mastered basic Korean terminology. To understand taekwondo requires students to have a working knowledge of Korean culture and language. The language of taekwondo is an integral part of your training. All commands for punches, strikes, blocks, kicks, stances, and steps are delivered in Korean. You will learn the Korean vocabulary by associating the movements with the commands. Use the glossaries in this chapter to give you a head start.

CHAPTER

4

FALLING

AND ROLLING

ne of the most important skills anyone can possess, martial artist or not, is the proper technique for falling. Children take falling in stride and recover fairly quickly from a little spill. However, adults are much more rigid and inflexible than children, and for them, falling can be catastrophic—even life-threatening. Despite the fact that any one of us can fall at any time, we do very little to prepare ourselves for such an inevitable experience. One of the first responsibilities of a good taekwondo school is to teach the novice student how to fall.

It may take a new student weeks, or even months, to feel comfortable with some of the intricate techniques of a martial art. The blocks (maggi), kicks (cha-gi), and forms (poomse) may all serve to confuse new students, especially if they have been removed from physical activity for a while. But even the most uncoordinated students can learn how to fall and roll well enough to greatly reduce the chances of severe injury.

TECHNIQUE TIPS

1. Remain relaxed through the duration of your fall or roll.
2. Practice on a soft surface, such as on a mat or outdoors on grass.
3. Begin practicing falls and rolls only inches from the mat to minimize impact.
4. Tuck your chin on all of your falls and rolls.
5. Intentional falls or rolls result in point deductions in taekwondo tournament competition.

FALLING

Early in your martial arts career you will be introduced to the techniques of breakfalling. Practice breakfalling (and all techniques) with the supervision of an experienced instructor. However, if you choose to attempt any of these techniques on your own, be sure to practice on a mat.

FRONT BREAKFALL

The first breakfall you will probably learn is the front breakfall. To practice, start on your knees at the edge of the mat, facing the full length of the mat. Hold your body straight, with your hands about shoulder height, your elbows bent, and your palms facing away from you. (You can also cross your arms in front of your chest as shown here; just be sure your arms are parallel when you hit the mat.) The distance between your two palms should be a little less than shoulder width. Now fall forward onto the mat and land on your palms and forearms. It is imperative that you keep your palms about a fist's distance apart as you slap the ground below you with the whole palm and forearm as one unit. Do not bend your wrist, because it may break under the stress of the fall. Be sure to turn your head to one side and to keep your belly and chest off the ground, because glass or dirt from on the ground might get into your eyes if you look down as you breakfall. After considerable practice you'll feel comfortable with this movement, and you can move to the low crouch position.

The low crouch position resembles that of a baseball catcher, sitting low with the feet a little less than shoulder width apart and the knees bent and hands up. To practice breakfalls from this posture, move more toward the center of the mat. Push your legs back and spread them wide, landing on the balls of your feet as you fall forward on your palms and forearms. Keep the upper torso and knees off the ground and be sure to turn your head. After several weeks of practice, you can stand fully upright to practice the front breakfall.

REAR BREAKFALL

The next breakfall you'll learn is the rear breakfall. Practice impeccable form to reduce the chance of injuring the back of your head. Start near the edge of the mat with your back facing the length of the mat. Crouch into the baseball catcher's posture as you did in the front breakfall, but this time cross your arms in front of your chest. Begin by lowering your rear end to the mat as if you were going to sit, then continue to roll onto your back. Be sure to keep your chin tucked into your chest to keep from hitting your head. As you roll onto your back, point your legs toward the ceiling and slap the ground with your forearms and palms to neutralize and disperse the energy from the breakfall. Do not allow your arms to move beyond a 45-degree angle to the side or your body. The greater the angle, the more stress the shoulders get. After you have become comfortable with the breakfall from the low crouch position, begin practicing it from a standing posture.

SIDE BREAKFALL

The final breakfall you will learn as a beginner is the side breakfall to both the left and right sides of the body. This breakfall is the one most often seen in martial arts movies. Start to practice the side breakfall from the low crouch posture. Start in the middle of the mat with both hands at shoulder level, as with the front breakfall. This time, if you are doing a left side breakfall, drag your left leg in front of your right foot. Bend your right knee to lower yourself to the ground on your left side (not on your back), extend your left arm to a 45-degree angle to the side, and bring your right hand to your belly. Be sure to tuck your chin to your chest, to break your fall with your upper body, and to not slap the ground with your extended leg because it can sustain serious injury. To practice this breakfall from the right side, start from the same initial position and reverse the directions for each step.

ROLLING

Along with the basic breakfalls, you'll learn the two basic rolls: the forward roll and the backward roll. Rolling helps prevent injury when your momentum is too great to allow a breakfall, such as when you are shoved or kicked with considerable force.

FORWARD AND BACKWARD ROLL

To practice the forward roll, start at the edge of the mat, facing its full length. Take a long step forward with either leg, and lower your center of gravity. (The closer you are to the ground, the easier it is to perform a roll.) If you stepped with the right foot, you should roll toward the right and place the right palm on the floor in front of the right foot. (If you stepped with your left foot to begin with, you'll follow the previous instructions with the opposite hands and feet.) Now tuck your chin to your chest and push over with both feet. Be sure to keep the extended arm muscles firm and roll to the

side to avoid hitting your head on the ground. Try to keep your body very tight and round as you roll, and avoid hitting a leg or arm onto the ground. Get up as fast as you can after the roll. Practice the forward roll until you are comfortable performing it from both sides.

To do the backward roll, start with your feet on the edge of a mat with your back facing the length of the mat. Take a step back with either leg and bring your hands to the center of your body at about shoulder height and two fists' distance from your chest to serve as a counterbalance. Bend the knee of the leg you stepped back with and lower your rear end to the ground. Now as your rear touches the ground, tuck your chin to your chest, round your back, and kick over with the opposite leg. You'll be rolling over the shoulder of the same side that you stepped back with, so be sure to turn your head to one side.

An important part of this roll is to bring the leg you kick with toward the shoulder you are rolling over. For example, if you step back with your right leg, you roll over your right shoulder and kick your left leg toward your right shoulder.

CHAPTER

5

STANCES

aekwondo stances (sogi) are the foundation for all attacks and defenses. The power in your technique comes from your legs and hips. A strong base of support allows you to absorb an attack and to hit harder. When you strike or kick, a powerful force is generated equally in both directions. To hit through a target, shift your weight and relax into a rock-solid stance. Each stance is designed to provide you with a solid base as well as to develop power in your legs and hips. Stances are easy to learn but difficult to sustain when exhausted. Different stances are required for different moves. You can use some stances for many techniques, but others are specific to a particular strike. There are many different stances in taekwondo, and we explain in this chapter the most common ones. Practice moving into each stance (except for the attention stance) from the ready stance. The text will describe how you an position your arms once you have mastered the leg placement of each stance, but most of the photos in this chapter will show the hands on the hips to avoid distraction. Hold each stance for 30 seconds, then proceed to the next; add 15 seconds per week until you can hold each stance for three minutes.

TECHNIQUE TIPS

1. Practice stances often until you can perform each of them without thinking.
2. Maintain perfect posture: eyes up, back straight, shoulders even, stomach in, buttocks tucked under, and knees soft.
3. Look straight ahead and focus on your breathing.
4. Perform stance training at least three days per week.

ATTENTION STANCE

Place your feet together with your knees slightly bent and your arms to your sides. Look straight ahead, but don't focus on anything in particular. The attention stance (cha-ryot sogi) is used to show respect for senior students and instructors. The traditional bow starts from the attention stance, and all taekwondo movements begin from cha-ryot sogi.

READY STANCE

From your attention stance, move your left leg to the side until your feet are shoulder width apart. Keep your legs straight with your knees flexed slightly. At the same time bring your hands to your solar plexus and down to waist level. Do all movements simultaneously. At the conclusion of the action, tense your muscles. Keep your muscles tense until you begin your next effort. A casual version of the ready stance (joonbi sogi) may be used in a self-defense situation. Taekwondo competitors use the ready stance for both poomse and fighting.

HORSE STANCE

Stand with your feet twice shoulder width apart, toes pointed straight ahead, and your legs slightly bowed as if you were riding a horse. Sit down into your stance by bending your knees over your toes. Squeeze the cheeks of your buttocks and contract your abdominal muscles, hold your back straight, and focus your eyes straight ahead. Keep your arms bent with your hands in fists held close by your side. A variety of self-defense and competition techniques start from the horse stance (juchoom sogi), including the front punch, knife hand strike, and back fist strike.

BACK STANCE

Switch your feet from the ready stance to a right-foot-forward back stance (dwi-gubi sogi) by sliding your left foot back two feet and turning it perpendicular to your right foot with your toe pointing out. Trace a perfect ninety-degree angle with your feet. Bend both knees and maintain exemplary posture, with 70 percent of your weight on your back leg. Keep your elbows slightly bent with your fists protecting your groin. The back stance is a very strong defensive position because from it you may throw a front leg counterattack or rear arm punch without telegraphing your intentions. Taekwondo poomse often use back stances. An informal, shorter back stance is advantageous in self-defense. Simply bring your back foot half the distance toward your front foot.

FRONT STANCE

From the ready stance step straight back with the right foot so your feet are shoulder width apart to form a front stance (ahp-gubi sogi). Bring your right foot behind your left foot with both feet pointing straight ahead. A good front stance is as wide as it is long. Bend your front knee to a 90-degree angle and keep your back leg straight but not locked. Hold your stomach in, your back erect, your arms to your sides with your elbows slightly bent, and your hands in fists. Most offensive fighting techniques are thrown from this stance. Both front and rear hand strikes as well as rear leg kicks may be executed effectively from the front stance. But because your body is open to a frontal attack, this stance is not prudent for self-defense.

WALKING STANCE

From the ready stance, step back slightly into a walking stance (ahp sogi) so the toe of your right foot is even with the heel of your left foot. Relax your arms and hands comfortably at your sides. Use the walking stance to move ahead without telegraphing your intentions. You'll perform many blocks and attacks from the walking stance. Ahp sogi is useful in some self-defense situations because it isn't an aggressive stance and it probably won't provoke your opponent.

FIGHTING STANCE

From the ready stance, turn both feet 45 degrees to the right and step back with your right foot. Your feet should be shoulder width apart with your weight equally distributed. Stay light on the balls of your feet to use either foot as a weapon. Stand slightly sideways to your opponent to make less of your body a target. Remain relaxed but focused. Hold your chin down and your elbows close to your body with your hands up, like a boxer does. From the fighting stance (gyo-rugi sogi), you can attack and defend with either hand or foot at any time.

SELF-DEFENSE TIPS

STANCES

We hope you will never be required to use your taekwondo skills to defend yourself. But if you are threatened, turn slightly sideways to your adversary to protect your knees, groin, stomach, throat, nose, and eyes. Rather than striking a martial arts pose, bring your feet a little less than shoulder width apart with your weight evenly distributed. Keep your knees slightly bent so you can readily kick with either leg. If you decide to defend yourself with your hands and arms, lower your center of gravity by bending your knees. When the action begins, bring your chin down to your chest and hold your arms in a fighting position.

ARM STRIKES

Strikes are formidable weapons. Your arms and hands are your quickest attack. Properly used, basic strikes (chi-gi) can disable an opponent. Elite taekwondoists can incapacitate an opponent with an elusive two-inch punch. Thrown incorrectly, however, a strike can injure your elbow, wrist, knuckles, or fingers.

Transfer your weight into your blows and stay balanced. On all strikes, stay relaxed, but keep your wrist firm. With the same force and speed you use for your strike, pull your nonstriking arm in the opposite direction to retain your balance and to prepare you to block or counterattack. Use your yell (ki-hop) to startle your opponent and increase the power of your strike. Resistance training can enhance the power and speed of your strikes (see chapter 13).

Pick a target but do not telegraph your delivery. Make no forward motion except when you initiate your attack. Cock your elbow the same way for every strike. If you prefer fighting from a distance and you have long arms, take advantage of the jab, backfist, palm heel, and knife hand strike. If you are stocky with shorter arms you may favor hooks, elbows, punches, and reverse punches. Practice all of your strikes with both arms so you may be more deceptive. Practice slowly at first; later you will strike with determination and without hesitation. The front punch, reverse punch, and hook punch to the body are the only strikes permitted in competition. In self-defense situations, deliver your strikes with malicious intent to an open target.

TECHNIQUE TIPS

1. Hit fast and hard to the target area.
2. Maintain a relaxed focus as you strike.
3. Relax your muscles until the moment of impact. Relaxed muscles allow you to move faster and expend less energy.
4. Think defense. Hit with a punch, but be prepared to block.
5. Snap your strikes and instantly retract them.
6. When rehearsing, imagine an opponent and picture yourself blasting your technique through the target.
7. Throw your strike while your opponent is busy thinking about attacking.
8. Use a mirror to study your form as you practice.

FRONT PUNCH

The front punch (ahp chi-gi) is one of the first strikes you learn in taekwondo. Begin in a horse stance. Make a fist with both hands by rolling your fingers tightly together to protect your hands and pressing your thumbs tightly against your index and middle fingers on the outside of your fists. With a piston-like motion, extend your left hand out to the front and pull your right arm back so your fist rests underneath your armpit. (The palm of your left hand faces the floor and the palm of your right hand faces the ceiling.) Retract your left hand while you forcefully extend your right fist, striking with the first two knuckles. Use this out-and-back movement for each repetition. A common error is to push your punch instead of thrusting it. Learn to relax so your arms feel like strings with fists attached. Your knees are soft and your back straight in a solid horse stance. Punches can be used to the body in competition and to the face, throat, solar plexus, and groin in self-defense situations.

HOOK PUNCH

You can deliver the hook punch (gullgi chi-gi) with your front or rear hand. Begin in a back stance, then pivot on the ball of your rear foot 90 degrees so that your feet finish in a modified front stance. As you pivot, bring your rear elbow up and parallel to the floor. Hit with your first two knuckles with your palm facing the floor at contact. Your hook is a solid assault from in close. The power in your hook comes from your hip. The hook punch is fast and deceptive, so keep it tight and don't swing wide. You can deliver the hook punch as a body attack in competition and to the head in self-defense.

JAB

The jab (ahp-joomock ji-roukee) is another fast strike with the front hand. It is not as powerful as the hook, but you can use it effectively for setting up another, more powerful blast such as a front kick or reverse punch. Begin in a fighting stance with your elbows bent and both fists up. Keep your elbows in close to guard your body. Extend your front fist forward to the target and hit with your first two knuckles. Twist the wrist of your striking hand so your palm is facing down at contact. Bring your hand back as quickly as you extended it. The jab does not have enough power to score in competition, but you might use it to lead off an attack to the face in a self-defense situation.

ELBOW STRIKE

The elbow strike (palkoop chi-gi) is a remarkably powerful technique that can be employed from a variety of angles: across into the face; back to the temple; straight up into the solar plexus; down to the face, throat, or collarbone; or directly behind you into the solar plexus or groin. Use it when you are too close to punch or kick. Begin in a fighting position, then twist your hips into a front stance and transfer your weight into the strike. Strike with either elbow. Cup your free hand over the fist of your striking arm for additional power. You may not use the palkoop chi-gi in competition, but it is excellent for self-defense.

KNIFE HAND STRIKE

To perform the knife hand strike (son-nal chi-gi), begin in a horse stance with both hands in fists and your palms facing your groin. Lift either hand to your ear as if preparing to throw a ball. Shoot it straight toward the neck of your imaginary opponent, twisting your hand just before contact so your palm faces upward. Strike with the meaty portion of the side of your hand—the part between the wrist and where your little finger joins your hand. As you strike with one hand, retract your other fist to rest underneath your armpit. Strike horizontally to the neck or vertically to the collarbone. Snap your wrist at the end of your attack for added speed and power. Son-nal chi-gi is useful for self-defense, but it is not permitted in competition.

PALM HEEL STRIKE

To execute the palm heel strike (ba-tang-son chi-gi), begin in a horse stance with your elbows in and your hands up in a fighting position. Either hand can be used to attack.The chin and solar plexus (shown here) are possible target areas to stun your attacker.The palm heel strike is a hard, bludgeoning blow that requires little physical strength to be successful. Add power to the palm heel strike by bringing your open hand up next to your ear with the palm facing forward and twisting your hips just prior to contact. Thrust your palm heel straight to the target. A surge of power will begin from your rear foot, travel through your body, and channel into the palm. The palm heel strike is a very effective

self-defense technique, but it is not allowed in competition. Another option in a life-threatening situation is to aim the lower part of your palm at the soft part of your opponent's nose to drive the nasal bone up at a 45-degree angle. Use this strike only in critical situations, because striking the nose in this manner could kill your assailant.

REVERSE PUNCH

The rear hand reverse punch (bandae ji-roukee) is the most powerful strike. It is a very graceful, flowing technique that uses your entire body. Start from a fighting stance, then pivot your rear foot into a front stance as you twist your hip to loose a power chain that explodes from out of your striking hand through the target. Your weight shifts from your rear foot to your front foot prior to contact. Remain relaxed until the moment of impact, and use the first two knuckles for penetration and a twist of the wrist for torque. Retract your nonstriking arm to create even more thrust. Rear hand techniques are slower than front hand strikes, but as

the reverse punch accelerates toward its target, it becomes more forceful. The reverse punch is an awesome weapon in a self-defense situation, targeting the solar plexus or face. In taekwondo competitions, it is the only hand strike that can score to the body with "trembling shock" (see chapter 12).

BACK FIST STRIKE

The back fist strike (dung-joomock chi-gi) is a fast, front hand technique thrown from a fighting or back stance. It is similar to a jab except that it moves horizontal to the target. Assume a fighting position with your elbows bent and your arms relaxed. Move your fist in a slapping motion toward your target. Be careful not to telegraph your intentions by lifting your elbow. Make contact with your first two knuckles, then retract your hand quickly so you may block or attack at will. You can use dung-joomock chi-gi in a self-defense situation as a leadoff technique to the head, but it is not permitted in taekwondo competitions.

BREAKING

TV Guide announced a televised martial arts demonstration featuring the breaking of a 600-pound block of ice. We waited days for the program to be aired, and when it finally came on, we couldn't believe our eyes. A heavy man was pacing back and forth in preparation to crush huge slabs of ice with a single elbow strike. As he approached the ice, the top slab broke the next slab, and that slab broke the next like dominoes. We couldn't tell who was more embarrassed—the host of the television program or the heavy guy.

Beginning students are sometimes disappointed to discover that the martial arts do not revolve around breaking boards and bricks. Bruce Lee said, "Boards don't hit back." Still, you may decide to perform some simple breaks to satisfy your curiosity and boost your confidence. Pick a dry pine board twelve inches long, twelve inches wide, and three-quarters of an inch thick. Have a partner hold the top and bottom of the board in the palms of her hands, squeezing tightly with her fingers so the board won't move. Your partner's elbows should be locked as she uses her shoulders for strength and support. This position will give you a clear shot at hitting the board dead center.

Make sure your partner holds the board with the grain of the wood lining up horizontally. Squeeze your dominant hand into a fist (a *hammer fist*) and concentrate all of your energy into hitting and continuing through the middle of the board. It will not hurt—unless, of course, the board doesn't break. Imagine your hand going through the board, then ki-hop loudly as you put all of your power into your strike. You may also break boards with any of the different kicks as well. To do so, strike the board with the heel, ball, or knife edge of your foot.

SELF-DEFENSE TIPS

ARM STRIKES

You must think fast and be fast in a self-defense situation. Arm strikes are your best weapons for a quick, all-out assault. Your legs provide you with a strong base of support, leaving your arms free to block and counter. If your opponent is within an arm's length, attack with a jab, backfist, or palm heel to the nose. If he is too close to extend your arm, throw a short reverse punch, hook punch, or elbow strike to the face, solar plexus, or throat. If an assailant sneaks up from behind, use your elbows if he is close, or spin and lash out with a backfist if he is at arm's length. Hit fast and hard. Follow up with finishing strikes if necessary.

CHAPTER

7

KICKS

icks (cha-gi) are your most powerful weapons. Kicks are fast, like arm strikes, but they can be thrown from a further distance. Your feet are more resilient than your hands, but kicks require more energy to deliver, they lessen your balance, and you lose your advantage if your kick is caught.

Most kicks can be broken down into four easy steps: (1) foot up, (2) foot out, (3) foot back, and (4) foot down. Initially, speed and power are not relevant; walk through the motions emphasizing precision. Kick with your hip (by pivoting your supporting foot so your heel points toward your target) for added power. Kick without your hip (which requires no pivot or hip twist) for speed. Later you can focus on the position of your feet, knees, toes, and upper body.

Before you extend your kick, raise your knee as high as you can to shield yourself (chambering). Keep your back straight until the last possible moment so you do not telegraph your intentions, then fire your foot to the target. Chamber your knee in the same way for the roundhouse kick, side kick, and hook kick. Keep your supporting knee bent slightly to maintain your balance. Practice consecutive double and triple kicks holding your knee high. The section in chapter 13 called "Kick Resistance Training" will aid you in your multiple-kick training.

Chambering.

If your legs are long and lanky and you have good flexibility, you can use many different kicks in your arsenal of attacks. People with short, stocky body frames may find the front kick, side kick, and back kick useful if they can get within range of their opponent; especially if they extend their hip into each kick. In competition, snap your kicks to the upper body and head of your opponent. If you have limited flexibility, thrust your kicks low and hard.

Practice your kicks from different stances. Learn to throw every kick from either leg and from any stance to maintain deception. Learn the front, roundhouse, side, back, axe, swing, and crescent kicks first. After you've practiced them for a few weeks, try the hook kick. Practice each kick slowly until you learn proper form.

TECHNIQUE TIPS

1. Walk on the knife edge (baalnul) of your feet with your foot turned in to strengthen your ankles for your kicks.
2. Stabilize your arms to block or counter after your kicks.
3. Retract your foot as quickly as you threw it.
4. Extend your hip to increase the power in your kicks.

FRONT KICK

Learn the front kick (ahp cha-gi) in four steps. Begin in a fighting stance. Raise your rear foot to your knee and point your kicking knee to your target, being sure to chamber the heel of your kicking foot as close to your hip as possible. Extend your foot to the target, pull your toes back, and strike with the ball of the foot. Quickly bring your foot back to your knee to protect yourself against a counterattack. Finally, set your foot down on the floor in a controlled fashion. Kick to the shin, knee, or groin in a self-defense situation using the tip of your shoe, ball of your foot, or top of your foot. In competition, strike with the ball of your foot or your heel to the face, chest, or abdomen.

ROUNDHOUSE KICK

The roundhouse kick (dolryo cha-gi) is another four-step technique. Begin in a fighting stance. Raise your rear leg so that the side of your knee is parallel to the floor and chamber your heel close to your hip. Snap the foot from the folded position horizontally to the target, striking with the ball of your foot, top of your foot, or with your toe if you are wearing hard shoes, and twisting your hips for added power. Pull your foot back to your knee as if you were cracking a whip. Put your foot back on the floor to resume the fighting stance. A roundhouse kick is an excellent way to close the gap and put you on the offensive. They are fast, deceptive, and powerful. Roundhouse kicks are the most frequently used techniques in taekwondo competitions. Most competitors use the top of the foot as the striking surface. Roundhouse kicks may score to the kidney area, front of the body, and the head. A roundhouse kick to the groin or thigh is an excellent self-defense strategy.

SIDE KICK

There are four steps to the side kick (yop cha-gi). Begin in a fighting stance. Pivot on your front foot, raise your rear knee to chest level, and chamber your foot in a position that protects your groin. Keep your back upright until the last second and then extend your foot, fast and hard, straight to the target, twisting your hip for added power and slicing through the target with your heel. Retract your foot to your knee. Finally, set your foot down into position to resume a fighting stance. A front leg side kick aimed at the body of an attacking competitor is used regularly in competition as a defensive technique. In self-defense, direct a side kick to your attacker's shin or knee so you can remain sideways and protect your groin, knees, and abdomen.

BACK KICK

Execute the back kick (dwi cha-gi) in four stages. Begin in a ready stance. Raise your kicking foot to your knee as you look over the shoulder of your kicking leg. Keeping your eyes fixed on your opponent and using your hip for added power, thrust your heel straight back, keep your toes pointed down, and drive your heel through the target. After contact, retract your foot back to your knee. Rest your foot gently on the floor. The spinning back kick to the body, an advanced version of the back kick, scores in competition. If your opponent reels, throw a jump spinning back kick. But spinning back kicks are risky in the street because you turn your back to your adversary. If an assailant attacks from behind, throw a back kick straight to the groin, knee, shin, or top of his foot.

AXE KICK

You can accomplish the axe kick (nerya cha-gi) in two steps. Begin in a front stance. Raise your rear leg until you feel tension in the back of your leg. Pull from your hip and swing your foot down, striking with the back of your heel. Imagine taking a giant step; your foot hammers down on your opponent. Maintain your hands in position to block or strike. Because the axe kick is relatively slow, your attacker may catch your foot or jam the kick; use the axe kick to strike only to the head in competition. Never attempt a kick to the face of an attacker in a self-defense situation because he may grab your foot, you might slip, or you may be pushed off balance.

CRESCENT KICK (OUT TO IN)

The out to in crescent kick (ahn bandul cha-gi) may be performed in two stages. Begin in a fighting stance with your left foot forward. Swing your right leg, from your hip, out to the right side. When your leg reaches its peak, flex your ankle and hook your foot sharply toward your opponent's midline until you strike your intended target. Strike (from the outside perimeter of your opponent's body toward his midline) with the bottom of your foot. Keep both knees slightly bent throughout the kick. Your target is the face of your opponent; therefore, this technique is only valuable in competition. Switch legs and repeat.

CRESCENT KICK (IN TO OUT)

The in to out crescent kick (backat bandul cha-gi) is the opposite of the out to in crescent kick, and is also a two-step technique. Begin in a fighting stance with your left foot forward. Raise your right leg from your hip, but instead of bringing it from the outside to the inside, as with the out to in crescent kick, hook it from the inside to the outside to contact your opponent's face with the back edge of your right heel. Keep both knees slightly bent. This kick is for competition only. Switch legs and repeat.

SIDE HOOK KICK

The side hook kick, usually thrown with the front leg, can be broken down into four steps. Begin in a fighting stance. Lift your front knee to your chest as if to execute a side kick. Bring your foot forward in an arc, hooking it horizontal to the target, and, with your back straight so as not to telegraph your intentions, strike with the back of your heel. Bring your foot back to the chambered position as quickly as you can. Set your foot down on the floor. The side hook kick is deceptive in competition because you chamber your foot exactly as you do in a side kick. Because your opponent's head is your only viable target, don't use the side hook kick for self-defense.

SELF-DEFENSE TIPS

KICKS

In a self-defense situation, aim your kicks low—to the shin, knee, and groin. If you kick above the waist, you might slip and fall or your attacker might catch your kick and send you hurtling to the ground. Strike fast and hard. Kick with the tip of your shoe, ball of your foot (ahp-chook), or your heel (dwi-chook). Keep your eyes focused on your opponent's solar plexus. Remain balanced so you do not telegraph your technique. Use kicks to set up finishing punches and strikes.

CHAPTER

8

BLOCKS

Blocks (maggi) are a last resort. If your opponent has moved close enough to attack, without your being able to counterattack, then block. Unlike the bone-on-bone power blocks exhibited in popular martial arts movies, blocking should be a smooth and effortless redirection of force—almost imperceptible.

Blocks redirect your opponent's energy so you may counterattack. You can't think about blocking; you must train yourself simply to react. But don't overreact—your opponent may throw a fake. Instead of concentrating on an attacking arm or leg, focus on your opponent's solar plexus so you can see his entire body with your peripheral vision. Leave no openings in your fighting position. Instead, make your attacker create one. Blocking your adversary's best techniques can frustrate him. You won't have time to move through a traditional block in a competitive or self-defense situation; however, train through the complete movement so you retain the basic motion. An abbreviated form of your block will come naturally. If your are practiciing alone, stand in front of a mirror and practice the blocks with each hand from a horse stance until they are second nature. If you are prcticing blocks with a partner, begin each block in a front or walking stance as shown in the photos in this chapter.

TECHNIQUE TIPS

1. Do not overreact to your opponent's attack; it may be a fake. Wait until your opponent commits himself, then block.
2. Redirect your opponent's attack and then counterattack.
3. Make your blocks quick, precise, and focused.
4. Retract the arm that's not blocking as you execute the block.
5. Twist your hips for power on each block.
6. As you're learning, emphasize form as you throw each block. Later, increase the speed and power of the block.
7. Study the photos to see ideal blocking form. Practice blocks slowly until you can duplicate what you see in the pictures.

MIDDLE OUTER BLOCK

Begin the middle outer block (backat maggi) in the front stance with your hands in fists and your palms facing your groin. When your opponent attacks with his left fist, cross your right arm under your left while you twist your hip in the direction of the block (this action can be reversed if the attack is coming from the right). Pivot your feet into a 45-degree-angle front stance. Bend your right elbow to make a 90-degree angle and snap your right arm forward so that the knuckles of your right hand are at eye level. Retract your left fist underneath your left armpit so your palm faces up a split-second before you block your opponent's body punch with your right arm. Stay relaxed throughout the movement, then tense your muscles at the completion of the block.

KNIFE HAND BLOCK

Begin the knife hand block (son-nal maggi) in a walking stance, palms open. Bring both arms up to your left shoulder, palms facing away from your body, and pivot your feet into a 45-degree-angle back stance. Stay sideways as you whip both arms forward to block. Knock the body punch away with your right hand, and guard your solar plexus with your left. Keep your elbows bent at 90 degrees. Stay relaxed throughout the movement. Then flex your muscles at the completion of the block.

To throw a low knife hand block, follow the instructions for the knife hand middle block; but instead of bringing your arms forward, extend them downward so that your right hand blocks a kick and finishes six inches above your thigh. Your left hand guards your solar plexus.

RISING BLOCK

Begin the rising block (wee maggi) in a short front stance with your hands in fists. Raise your right arm to block a face punch. Twist it so that as it reaches your forehead, your palm is facing your opponent. Retract your left fist underneath your armpit, rotating your palm so it faces up. Block fast and hard, but remain relaxed until the completion of the block.

MIDDLE INNER BLOCK

The middle inner block (ahn maggi) begins in a front stance with your hands in fists. Raise your right fist up to your ear, with your palm facing your opponent. Your elbow should be parallel to your shoulder. Twist your hips and pivot your feet into a 45-degree-angle front stance. Bring your arm sharply across your body, twisting your palm so it faces your midsection at the conclusion of the block. Retract your left fist underneath your armpit, and rotate your palm so it faces up as you block your opponent's body punch. Tighten your muscles at contact.

LOW BLOCK

Begin the low block (ahre maggi) in a walking stance with your hands in fists. Raise your right fist over your left shoulder with your palm facing your ear. Sweep your fist downward across your body, blocking with the outside of your forearm. Finish in a front stance with your elbow slightly bent and your fist six inches above your knee. Retract your left fist underneath your armpit, rotating your palm so it faces up, as you block your opponent's kick to your lower body. Relax all of your muscles until contact.

X-BLOCK

Begin the X-block (yeot pero maggi) from the front stance by shooting both arms forward at the same time and crossing them at the wrists to form an X. The blocking surface is the area between the wrists where the forearms cross. A high X-block (shown below) is a defense against downward attacks to the head, face, or shoulders. A low X-block, sometimes called a reinforced block, is a good defense against kicks to the lower body, especially to the groin. To perform a low X-block, thrust both fists down, crossing at your wrists to block a hard kick to your lower body. Time the block so your opponent's foot meets at the intersection of your arms. Use the X-block against kicks that are too powerful to be blocked with a single arm. Use the X-block only when you are certain of the placement of your opponent's attack. Both of your arms will be tied up, so it is very important that you don't get fooled trying to block a fake. Wait until you are sure of the attack before executing this block

SELF-DEFENSE TIPS

BLOCKS

If you have attempted every viable form of escape to no avail, and you believe you are about to be attacked, your best block is a counterattack. The moment you perceive an aggressive movement from your assailant, strike immediately. Beat your opponent to the punch.

If you are not able to strike immediately, keep your hands up and be ready to block an attack. Use a middle inner block to thwart a shove to your chest. A rising block may divert a punch away from your head, or a low block may be used to sweep away a knife attack. Maintain your balance and poise while you follow up with combinations, if necessary. When you are in control of the situation, run away.

CHAPTER

9

STEPS

Stepping is not flashy, but it is a building block to your tae-kwondo success. If you develop good stepping skills, you can launch techniques with maximum power. Anyone can throw a punch or kick; the individual who controls the distance between himself and his opponent prevails. Stepping requires a tremendous amount of discipline.

Step, then throw your body weight into the prescribed punch, kick, block, or strike. Move briskly from one step to the next. Hold your center of gravity low to preserve your balance. Your head, shoulders, and hips align on the same plane. To remain aligned and balanced throughout your steps, bend your knees slightly so that if you were to drop a string from the top of your knee, it would hit your toe. Move silently without dropping your feet. Stay out of reach of your opponent, and take advantage of openings.

Sometimes you will step quickly to attack, with grace and speed allowing you to hit before your opponent can react. However, speed is not everything—timing is. If you are not genetically endowed to throw techniques with blinding force, you can use your first step as a fake to set up another step. Shuffle and wait for a reaction from your opponent. If your opponent does not react, score with a punch or kick. If he attempts to counter your shuffle, add a step and then strike to an open target.

Correct stepping improves the balance, speed, and power of your technique. You can step forward, backward, or from side to side. Be prepared to attack or defend during each step. Practice footwork in front of a mirror to examine your form, improve your deception and timing, and develop new strategies.

TECHNIQUE TIPS

1. Maintain excellent posture by holding your shoulders, hips, and eyes level through your steps, focusing your eyes on your imaginary opponent.

2. Slide your stepping foot close to the floor and maintain bent knees throughout the step.

3. Step lightly on the balls of your feet—front, back, side to side—as though you're on eggshells.

4. Change your footwork on attacks. Your opponent will have difficulty designing a counter. Shuffle, step, push slide, or jump.

5. Jumping rope, sparring, and shadow boxing improve your stepping efficiency.

SHUFFLE FORWARD OR BACKWARD

Begin in a horse stance with your left foot closest to your opponent. As quickly as you can, slide your right foot to your left foot by gripping the floor with the ball of your left foot and pulling your right foot forward, then push off with your right foot to propel your left foot forward again while facing sideways to your opponent. When you finish your right foot has replaced the original position of the left foot and your left foot has advanced a shoulder's width. Keep your shoulders and hips level and your knees bent. If you stay level, your opponent will find it more difficult to perceive your motion. Use the shuffle forward to close the gap between you and your opponent. Shuffle backward to retreat. Whether you are in competition or the street, be sure that your hands remain in a fighting position throughout your step. Remember to practice with both sides.

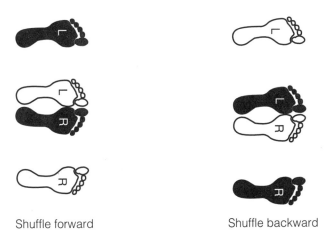

Shuffle forward   Shuffle backward

Starting position   Ending position

FORWARD OR BACKWARD STEP

Begin in a front stance with your hands in a fighting position. For the forward step, shift your rear leg in toward your front knee and then out and forward in a semicircular fashion until you have formed another front stance with the stepping foot forward. Move your rear knee slightly inward to protect your groin as you prepare for your next movement. Your knees remain slightly bent to stay level. Reverse the procedure to retreat. Balance a book on top of your head to practice staying level while stepping.

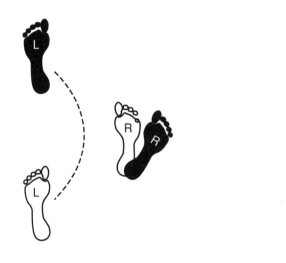
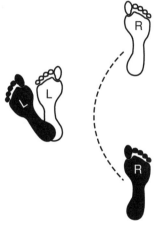

Forward step   Backward step

Starting position   Ending position

PUSH SLIDE FORWARD OR BACKWARD

The push slide is the most deceptive method of closing the gap. If you perform the slide correctly, your attack will hit your opponent before he is aware that you are close enough to strike. Start with your feet in a short horse stance with your left foot closest to your opponent and your hands in a fighting position. Raise your left knee, and let it pull you toward your opponent as your right foot slides along the floor. Come to rest in another horse stance with your left foot forward. To move backward, bring the right foot slightly off the floor and let it pull you back. Keep both knees bent throughout the movement. Keep your shoulders level and your arms fixed so you won't telegraph your intentions. The push slide is the quickest and most elusive stepping strategy for both self-defense and competition. Remember to practice on both sides.

Push slide forward   Push slide backward

Starting position   Ending position

SWITCH FEET

Begin in a fighting stance with your left foot and your left arm forward in a fighting position. Twist your hips quickly while jumping slightly and switch your feet into a right-foot-forward fighting stance. At the same time, pull your right arm forward. Your feet should barely leave the floor, and your arms simply switch. Keep your shoulders and hips level throughout and your eyes on your opponent. Switching feet gives you a new perspective on your competitor and allows you to try different methods of attack.

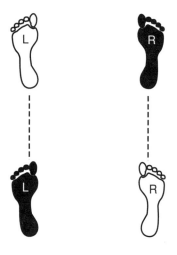

Starting position   Ending position

CHAPTER

FORMS

A *form* (poomse) is a specific pattern of movements. Poomse allow students to practice defensive and offensive movements alone against an imaginary opponent. The movements include combinations of the basic stances, blocks, strikes, and kicks. The practice of forms is generally considered the most important element in the development of proper taekwondo technique, and students learn a new form with each progressive belt level. Practitioners learn poomse step by step, from uncomplicated, easy ones to complex, difficult ones. In most schools students learn their first form at the yellow belt level and are expected to learn a new form and improve their performance of the previous one with each progressive belt promotion.

Poomse teach students to coordinate their mind and body and force them to move their upper and lower body simultaneously in a variety of directions. Because students are conscious of ending the poomse in a certain spot, they make subtle biomechanical adjustments to their movements which facilitate balance and distancing. In the beginning students are also attentive to their breathing. They force themselves to breath out with each technique and eventually can do so without thought or effort.

Forms are vital to students' development in the martial arts, and virtually all taekwondo schools teach poomse as part of their curriculum. Some schools may focus exclusively on sparring, but this approach is very limiting and deprives the student of a well-rounded education in taekwondo. Students who train in the WTF Olympic style of taekwondo will be required to memorize and perform the eight poomse of the Tae Geuk series. The eight Tae Geuk forms, which are based on a different Taoist principle of nature, such as heaven and earth, are more than just random combinations of movements. Each movement within the form has a specific purpose and meaning for the taekwondo student, such as reinforcing how to launch a counterattack or block attacks to various areas of the body. See the sample poomse later in this chapter for a description of each movement and its meaning for form one in the Tae Geuk series.

PRACTICING POOMSE

In the beginning of practice, focus on the physical elements of learning a new poomse. The most fundamental thing you need to learn is the order of the movements of the particular poomse in the series you are learning. Each movement consists of a stance and a block, a strike, or a kick. Know how to execute each one of the basic techniques, such as a forward stance or front kick, before attempting to learn an entire poomse.

Begin each poomse in the ready stance. The first movement is a turn of the head in the direction your first turn or step will be. In fact, every time the form requires a change of direction, you must first look toward that direction. Most forms are designed to begin and end in the same spot, so it is up to you to space your stances so you finish in the original position. To accomplish this difficult task, you need balance and grace. Any uneven or unnecessary steps will throw off your spacing.

When you're familiar with all the movements of the poomse, start refining the form by concentrating on timing and transitions. The *timing* of a poomse refers to the pace at which you execute the moves. A good guideline is to take a full second between each movement. A *transition* is a smooth change in direction. For example, in the first Tae Geuk form, the student moves from a forward stance to the front into a walking stance,

and then into a rising block to his left. Awkward, off-balance transitions can make your form look sloppy. To help in smooth transitions, practice sliding your foot, rather than stepping, into a new stance.

Another important element of proper poomse is accurately striking targets with focus and power. Each strike in a form is directed to a specific, vital point on the opponent's body, such as the solar plexus, groin, and so on. Keep the targets in mind when doing the poomse. Strikes and kicks are useless unless the student is aware of the target and throws it with the proper speed and power. A poomse is a training tool, and you should be conscious of what kinds of strikes are required for each vital spot. However, in most instances it is not sufficient to just touch a vital area. Instead, strike with good focus and power, imagining that your life depends on the result of the strike. When doing techniques in the air, relax and snap the technique like a whip. While performing poomse, think about breath control. Exhale with each strike, block, or kick. When throwing a kick or a punch to a vital spot, aim for the respective area on your own body as a reference point.

When practicing poomse, focus on each of the essential elements in turn, such as on balance or power. To give you a good sense of your balance and focus, test yourself by practicing the poomse with your eyes closed or in a dark room. After you have a sense of the elements, you can integrate them into a unified performance.

Poomse practice can also help improve your self-defense skills. A poomse is designed to constantly change direction—it's not just for beauty and showmanship. The changes in direction in a poomse simulates multiple attackers from various angles. Repeat the form over and over to drill the techniques into your muscle memory. Also practice specific pieces of the poomse over and over again. The only way to develop instinctive, reflexive responses is through constant repetition. However, the repetition won't help you unless you believe you are facing real opponents. Repetition will also help develop your cardiovascular endurance. Practice the poomse 15 to 20 times without stopping and at full tilt. If done correctly and with the right attitude, the poomse is your greatest training tool.

The physical movements of the poomse are only part of the picture. To completely master poomse, you need to understand the mental aspects, too. Most of the movements in the Tae Geuk forms are short and simple—only about 18 to 20 movements—so you can memorize them with a little practice. However, memorizing the moves by no means suggests that you've perfected the form. A poomse is much more than a choreographed dance routine. Proper execution of a poomse resembles meditation in motion. The poomse should breathe with the spirit of the student performing it. Make the poomse a personal expression of yourself. A shallow, robotic performance of the movements completely misses the point of doing poomse. To achieve a better understanding of the meaning of the Tae Geuk series, practice the forms as a whole set. You don't have to practice them in a particular order, but do practice them in a continuous series without any breaks.

POOMSE COMPETITION

Tournaments give you an excellent opportunity to compete with and learn from your peers. Most competitions feature sparring, board breaking, and poomse competitions, and in competition poomse will be judged on correct and orderly execution of each movement and on your degree of proficiency in their execution. Proficiency is evaluated with the following criteria:

- Beginning and ending at the same spot
- Executing powerful and speedy techniques by tensing and relaxing muscles at the proper moment
- Mental concentration
- Focused eye and head movements
- Accurate targets
- Inhaling and exhaling at the proper moment
- Balance
- Rhythm and synchronization of movement.

SAMPLE POOMSE

To give you an idea of the types of movements required in a form, this section describes the techniques that comprise the Tae Geuk El-Jong, the first form of the Tae Geuk series.

Movement 1: Turn 90 degrees to the left, moving your left foot forward into a left walking stance, and execute a low block with the left arm.
Meaning: Defense against an attack to the mid-section.

Movement 2: Step forward with the right foot into a right walking stance and execute a mid-section punch with the right fist.
Meaning: Counterattack.

Movement 3: Turn 180 degrees to the right, step with the right foot into a right walking stance, and execute a low block with the left arm.
Meaning: Defense against an attack to the mid-section.

Movement 4: Step forward with the left foot into a left walking stance and execute a mid-section punch with the left fist.
Meaning: Counterattack.

Movement 5a: Step 90 degrees to the left with the left foot into a left forward stance and execute a low block with the left arm.
Meaning: Defense against an attack to the lower section.

Movement 5b: Remain in the left forward stance and execute a mid-section punch with the right fist.
Meaning: Immediate counterattack.

Movement 6: Step 90 degrees to the right with the right foot into a right walking stance and execute a middle block to the inside with the left arm.
Meaning: Defense against an attack to the mid-section.

Movement 7: Step forward with the left foot into a left walking stance and execute a mid-section punch with the right fist.
Meaning: Counterattack.

Movement 8: Step 180 degrees left with the left foot into a left walking stance and execute a middle block to the inside using the right arm.
Meaning: Defense against an attack to the mid-section.

Movement 9: Step forward with the right foot into a right walking stance and execute a mid-section punch with the left fist.
Meaning: Counterattack.

Movement 10a: Step 90 degrees to the right with the right foot into a right forward stance and execute a low block with the right arm.
Meaning: Defense against an attack to the lower section.

Movement 10b: Remain in the right forward stance and execute a mid-section punch with the left fist.
Meaning: Immediate counterattack.

Movement 11: Step 90 degrees to the left into a left walking stance and execute a rising block with the left arm.
Meaning: Defense against a downward attack to the head.

Movement 12a: Keeping the left foot in place, execute a mid-section front kick with the right foot.
Meaning: Initial counterattack or set-up strike.

Movement 12b: Step down with the right foot into a right walking stance and execute a mid-section punch with the right fist.
Meaning: Finishing counterattack.

Movement 13: Step 180 degrees to the right into a right walking stance and execute a rising block with the right arm.
Meaning: Defense against a downward attack to the head.

Movement 14a: Keeping the right foot in place, execute a mid-section front kick with the left foot.
Meaning: Initial counterattack.

Movement 14b: Step down with the left foot into a left walking stance and execute a mid-section punch with the left fist.
Meaning: Finishing counterattack.

Movement 15: Step 90 degrees to the right with the left foot into a left forward stance and execute a low block with the left arm.
Meaning: Defense against an attack to the lower section.

Movement 16: Step forward with the right foot into a right forward stance and execute a mid-section punch with the right fist while yelling "Ki-hop."
Meaning: Strong counterattack.

Finish the form by turning 180 degrees to the left, pivoting on the right foot to end in a ready stance.

Don't become so obsessed with winning trophies and medals that you lose sight of the purpose of poomse training. Forms practice helps you to grow and develop, but only if you're willing to constantly push yourself to improve. Even when you've earned a new belt and a new poomse to practice, continue to review the previous forms. A good student never forgets the basics. Return to your foundation and always work hard to improve it. You can always do even the most elemental poomse a little smoother or a little sharper.

CHAPTER

11

TACTICS

Develop tactics that utilize your strengths and protect your weaknesses. Adopt your own special strategies that you can count on in almost any situation. If you are blessed with extreme flexibility, spend hours in front of a mirror honing your special kick. If you are a quick stepper, practice closing the gap and striking without being blocked or countered. Use these movements spontaneously rather than responding predictably to an attack. Be innovative. Develop subtle changes in combinations and strategies, because you won't win by repeating the same techniques over and over.

Every opponent is different. One is tall, while another is short. One is heavy; another is thin. It takes practice to be able to move in any direction as you react to an opponent. You must work at controlling the distance between your opponent and you and the timing of your moves. Rehearse the combinations and counterattacks in this chapter until you can respond without thinking. React instinctively; by the time you think about reacting, it's too late to be effective.

BASIC STRATEGY

Whether you are defending your life or your championship title, you have several elements to consider. Practice the same way you execute. Don't joke around. Concentrate. Take a good look at your opponent to find a weakness. Be able to adjust to the style of each opponent. If you fight an opponent who is faster, stronger, and more flexible than you are, be smarter. If he is shorter and stockier than you are, keep your distance. Pepper him with kicks when he attempts to close the gap, but don't throw them right away. In competition, if you have excellent flexibility, hit hard and low at first; then, when your opponent brings his hands down to block, throw your favorite kick to the head. If he is tall and skinny, move inside his kicks. Jam him, and throw hard shots to the body.

In tournament competition, use deceptive footwork to set up a score. If footwork doesn't do it, throw a fake kick to belt level, and when your opponent brings her hands down to block, hit high. Be sure your fake kick seems real so your opponent attempts to block. If she doesn't react to your fake, score with a low kick. If she does bring her arm down, extend your foot so it makes contact with your opponent's arm before you slide your foot up to the head. If you are stunned, show no pain. Let the contact energize you to counterattack. Sometimes you must take risks to succeed. Don't try to save energy for your next fight, because there might not be one.

DISTANCE, TIMING, AND GAZE

All great fighters have the ability to control distance. You will never lose in a tournament or self-defense situation if you can regulate the amount of space between you and your opponent. Many good fighters can throw exemplary punches and kicks, but the elite are masters of commanding distance. Controlling distance means slipping away from or toward your opponent with impeccable timing. Ki-hop loudly and focus your eyes on the middle of your opponent's body (the solar plexus) so you can sense a hand or foot movement. Although your eyes should be trained on your opponent's solar plexus, your peripheral vision can also be used to detect attacks. Don't become too focused on one spot. You can also counterattack better when you evade your opponent's techniques by moving. Move just far away from your opponent so you don't get hit, then return with your counterattack.

STRIKING TACTICS

Choose an open target, and if none is available, create one. Throw a fake to establish an opening. If your opponent doesn't block the fake, turn the fake into a strike. If he does try to block it, you have your opening. For example, if you throw a fake to your opponent's head and he raises his arm to block it, strike to his side. If he remains flat on his feet, move him by shuffling from side to side or by attacking directly. During close-in fighting, there is no time to think. Let your fists find their targets. Don't try to hit so hard you lose your balance, because overextending causes you to lose your advantage. Control your attack by keeping your center of gravity over your hips. If you miss with any technique, recover to an upright position immediately. If your opponent bounces, strike when he is in the air; for that split second it is impossible for him to counterattack. Jam your opponent by stepping into his attack, especially during a spinning attack, and following up with a strike to his body.

KICKING TACTICS

You can deceive your opponent if you use your front foot to initiate attacks. Think low; throw high, and vice-versa. By thinking about attacking low, your body language will signal your opponent to drop his hands a bit. If your opponent is holding his hands low, snap a kick to the head. High hands call for a low attack. Hold your back erect when launching a kick and lean into your attack following your kick. Use your initial attack to close the gap; let your body find the target. Hit with a double kick—low-to-high or high-to-low—if your opponent blocks your first kick. Maintain concentration after hitting, for at that moment you are open to a counterattack. Focus on your opponent's solar plexus to perceive all movement with your peripheral vision. Always defend while attacking. Don't let up on the offensive, or the momentum will shift to your opponent.

If you and your opponent are deadlocked, kick low and hard to create an opening. Fake a spin kick to observe how your opponent reacts. Throw some slow attacks, then erupt with a sudden assault to catch your opponent off guard. When throwing a rear leg kick, hold your hands up to cover against a possible counter-attack. Use risky techniques such as jump front, side, or back kicks only when your rival is off-balance or back pedaling so you are not countered while in a vulnerable position.

COMBINATIONS

Combinations are a minimum of two techniques blended with grace, speed, and power into a sequence of strikes and kicks. The movements flow. Combinations are useful in competition or for self-defense, they look good, and they develop muscular endurance. You can choose from hundreds of different combinations to find the ones that work for you. Synthesize techniques to meet the needs that your size, strength, speed, and flexibility dictate. If your initial attack is blocked, look for an opening. A fast front hand jab can start the action. Your rear leg roundhouse kick may be your most powerful weapon, but set it up with a reverse punch. A general precept is to use your hands to set up your kicks and your feet to set up your punches. When an opening presents itself, fill it with a kick or a punch. Take a serious look at your strengths and weaknesses. You might find some combinations in the next few paragraphs that meet your needs. First try the front kick, jab combination, then progress to the more difficult combinations. Practice combinations exactly as you'd use them in combat.

Different combinations are effective depending on your opponent's reactions. If you attempt a front kick to the body and your opponent moves his arm downward to block, change your front kick to a roundhouse kick and score to an open target. Always stay a step ahead of your opponent.

TECHNIQUE TIPS

1. Twist your hips on your punch to set up your kick.

2. Attack from angles, not always directly.

3. Follow hands with feet, and vice-versa.

4. Throw one-two combinations rather than pausing; the opening will present itself.

5. Snap your kicks back rapidly so you can throw double and triple kicks.

6. Prepare another technique if your initial strategy doesn't score.

7. Modify combination techniques to fit your body, tailoring each combination to meet the needs of your unique physique, personality, and fighting situation.

FRONT KICK, JAB

Start this useful basic combination with your left hand and left leg forward in a fighting stance. Execute a right leg front kick and step forward. Keep your hands up in a fighting position. When your right foot touches the floor, throw a jab with your right hand. Use the front kick to lower your opponent's guard so you can deliver the jab cleanly. Practice this drill with your right leg forward in a front stance, too.

JAB, PUNCH, ROUNDHOUSE KICK

From a fighting stance, throw a jab with your front hand to create an opening for a reverse punch. If your adversary manages to block both strikes, snap a roundhouse kick to the open target. If she makes no attempt to block any one of your three attacks, hit with each of them. Flow from one move to the next so that your opponent will have difficulty blocking all three techniques. Practice to the other side of your body, too.

CRESCENT KICK, DOUBLE PUNCH

From a fighting stance, throw a rear leg crescent kick (in to out) to your opponent's head. Follow up immediately with a jab, punch combination. This technique is useful for competition. Be sure your opponent is not in a position to jam your initial kick. After you throw your crescent kick, lean into your punches for maximum power. Switch sides and repeat your practice.

JAB, PUNCH, CRESCENT KICK

From a fighting stance, snap a front hand jab followed by a rear hand reverse punch to the body. When your opponent brings his arms down to block, execute a crescent kick (out to in) to his head. This combination is useful for competition. Never use any kicking techniques to the head in a self-defense situation. During practice, switch sides and repeat.

PUNCH, PUNCH, KICK, PUNCH

Start with your left leg forward in a fighting stance. Throw a right reverse punch and pivot your right foot. Thrust a left punch. Snap a front kick with your right rear leg, and bring it back to your original stance. Explode with a final reverse punch with your right arm, twisting your hips into a front stance. Use this sequence as an aggressive, all-out blitz in competition or self-defense. Repeat with your other side when practicing.

COUNTERATTACKS

The purpose of a counterattack is to short-circuit your adversary's offense. Whenever your opponent attacks, you have an opening to counter. Anticipate hostile movements. Subtle shifts of the shoulders and hips reveal your aggressor's intentions. With experience, you can stop a malicious act with a simple strike. In most instances, you can thwart a hand assault with a kick. You can intercept and counter a foot attack with quick hands. In competition, however, kicks are the preferred method of attack and counterattack. The following counterattacks are just a sampling of the many possible responses to an opponent's attack.

TECHNIQUE TIPS

1. Don't take a shot directly. Let it sideswipe you. Turn away with your body, then counterattack (spin around, kick, and throw a punch).
2. Throw a defensive side kick into the opening created by your opponent's attack.
3. Develop a rock-hard torso so you won't fear a hit.
4. Practice body work (see chapter 13) to gain confidence in managing body shots.
5. Convert your retreat into a spinning back kick.
6. Use your arms as cushions, holding them close to your torso to block.
7. Avoid the punch to your head by moving your head out of the path of the oncoming blow. Slide in very close to your opponent (so close that there's skin on skin) or immediately counterattack.
8. If your opponent brandishes an explosive offense, allow him to introduce an assault, but jam it to frustrate his attack.

AXE KICK COUNTERED WITH REAR LEG ROUNDHOUSE KICK

When your opponent attempts an axe kick, shuffle step back to evade the attack and follow up with a rear leg roundhouse kick. Move just out of your opponent's reach so that you can counter immediately. Launch your roundhouse kick before your opponent's axe kick has reached the floor.

REAR LEG ROUNDHOUSE KICK COUNTERED WITH REAR LEG ROUNDHOUSE KICK

When your opponent throws a rear leg roundhouse kick, block it, and immediately follow up with a rear leg roundhouse kick. Anticipate your opponent's attack so that by the time it reaches you, your roundhouse kick is on its way. Use crushing speed and power to deliver this technique.

REAR LEG ROUNDHOUSE KICK COUNTERED WITH SPINNING BACK KICK

When your opponent attempts a rear leg roundhouse kick, block it, and immediately throw a spinning back kick to the open target. Be sure you have adequately blocked the roundhouse kick before attempting your spin. The timing of the block and counter is crucial to the success of this technique. Practice with a partner until your counterattack becomes automatic.

LEAN AWAY, DEFENSIVE SIDE KICK

When your opponent attacks with a punch, kick, or spinning technique, lean away, supporting all of your weight on your rear leg. Move just far enough to evade the assault, then throw a defensive side kick with your front leg. Timing is essential. Wait until your opponent commits his attack before you attempt to counter.

CRESCENT KICK COUNTERED WITH PUNCH

When your opponent attempts a crescent kick from close range, throw a reverse punch to the body. Your opponent's lifting his leg up for the crescent kick will allow you enough time to move in to counter. Use one arm to block and the other to throw a solid punch. This counterattack can be especially devastating because your attacker is off balance when you strike.

SELF-DEFENSE TIPS

COMBINATIONS AND COUNTERATTACKS

Blocks and stepping techniques work fine in competition, but it is better to beat your adversary to the punch in a self-defense situation. The moment your assailant begins his attack, strike straight, fast, and hard to an open target. Although you may be grazed by his attack, the force of your intercept strike should be the first step in your combination and counterattack. Blast forward with elbows, kicks, punches, and strikes. Do whatever it takes to stop the attack. There are no rules in the street. The following is a list of target areas that are especially effective for disabling and stopping an attacker.

TARGET AREA

❏ Chin   ❏ Groin   ❏ Neck   ❏ Solar Plexus

❏ Eyes   ❏ Kidneys   ❏ Nose   ❏ Top of Feet

❏ Ears   ❏ Knees   ❏ Shins

CHAPTER

12

COMPETITION

You will learn more about sparring in a few minutes of competition than you will in a lifetime in the dojang. Crowds, referees, judges, rules, and regulations bring forth an intensity that motivates and inspires. Not only must you adhere to strict rules and codes, but your weight is also scrutinized and your attitude is evaluated. If your bout with your opponent is close, you may be declared the winner if you show good sporting behavior. If you are equal to your rival in ability but she is more aggressive, she will win.

Competition is not just punching and kicking. Most elite taekwondo competitors agree that sparring requires as much mental skill as physical skill. But competitors spend little time mentally preparing for a competition. In this chapter, we teach you how to relax and to focus prior to stepping into the ring. You can follow the step-by-step imagery techniques to improve your performance in both sparring and poomse.

TOURNAMENT RULES

National and international matches have three rounds that last three minutes each, with one minute of rest between rounds. Local and regional tournaments may limit rounds to two minutes. Only same-sex matches are allowed. The ring is 8 meters (26 feet) by 8 meters, with a 12-meter (39 feet) by 12-meter out-of-bounds line (see below). Four corner judges, a head referee, and two jurors oversee the action. The head referee is responsible for the safety and discipline of the fighters. The referee moves around and stays close to the action. Whatever he says is law. Fighters cannot argue or talk back to the head referee. The four corner judges score each match. They record all infractions designated by the head referee. Local and regional corner judges use pads and pencils, while national and Olympic judges use electronic scoring systems to provide feedback that can be posted quickly at the end of each round. The jurors keep watch for any errors the head referee or four corner judges make. They also keep track, on a scoring sheet, of all point gains or losses. In case of a tie, the referee declares the winner.

Before the bout begins, the referee checks that each competitor is wearing a white, WTF-approved taekwondo uniform, shin and forearm pads, a groin guard, head gear, a mouth guard, and either a blue or a red chest protector (see next page). On the command of the head referee, the competitors bow to him, then to each other. They assume their fighting stances and await the head referee's

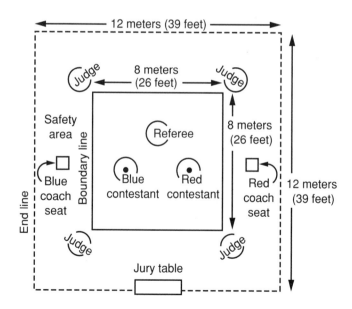

order to begin. The referee signals the end of the bout with a ceremonial bow.

SCORING

Only kicking and closed hand punching techniques score in Olympic-style sparring. No open-handed techniques or kicks with any area above the ankle joint can score. Fighting is continuous. You earn a point if you land a punch or kick with "trembling shock" to a proper target area (see next page) on your opponent's chest protector while you maintain perfect posture. You also score one point when you punch or kick an opponent's target area and he staggers or falls down. A kick to the head may also score. If you fall down or intentionally grab your opponent after an effective punch or kick, you won't score a point. You may not kick or strike below the belt. A knockout kick to the head can win a match, but punching to the neck or above is prohibited.

If a match is tied at the end of three rounds and one contestant has had more points deducted, the contestant who was awarded

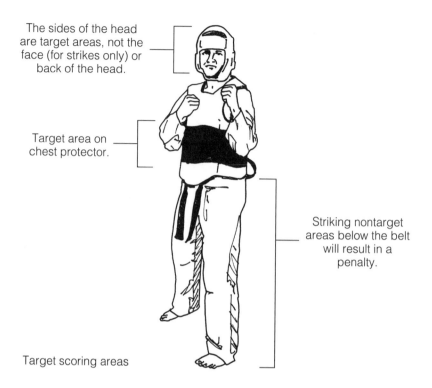

The sides of the head are target areas, not the face (for strikes only) or back of the head.

Target area on chest protector.

Striking nontarget areas below the belt will result in a penalty.

Target scoring areas

the most total points wins. If the score is tied and the point deductions are equal, the referee determines the winner based on the superiority of the techniques thrown. A technique that results in an 8-count knockdown is superior to any other. Kicks are superior to hand techniques, and jumping techniques are superior to standing techniques. In addition, kicks to the face score over kicks to the body, and counterattacks are superior to initiating attacks. If the referee can determine no clear winner from these criteria, she decides who she thinks was the most aggressive. Aggressiveness is displayed by putting your opponent on the defensive and initiating most of the attacks. If both competitors display all of the previous criteria equally, the referee may award the match to the fighter who exhibited the best sportsmanship.

Unsportsmanlike conduct such as attacking an opponent's face with the fist or faking pain are prohibited and will result in point deduction. If a contestant has three points deducted from his score, he loses the contest. Warnings and point deductions (see the sidebar on page 141) are enforced by the head referee.

$\mathcal{P}$OINT DEDUCTIONS

Two warnings (kyong-go) issued during the same round yield a one-point deduction. If a contestant receives an odd number of kyong-go penalties, the last penalty does not result in a point deduction. Warning penalties are given for the following infractions:

- Attacking the opponent's face with the fist
- Pushing the opponent down with the foot
- Intentionally falling to the floor
- Pushing with the hands, shoulders, or body
- Faking pain
- Stalling the contest
- Being forced out of the eight-by-eight boundary
- Grasping an opponent's uniform or body
- Attacking with the knees
- Escaping by turning your back to an opponent
- Moving out of bounds on purpose
- Attacking the groin or other nontarget area
- Intentionally kicking any part of the opponent's leg
- Gesturing to the judges to indicate a point was scored
- Offensive language and misconduct
- Throwing the opponent

A point is deducted immediately (gam-jeum) when a competitor does any of the following:

- Attacks after the head referee declares "break"
- Butts against the opponent's face or body
- Hurts an opponent's face with a fist
- Attacks an opponent who has fallen to the floor
- Attacks the back or back of head intentionally
- Moves out of the 12-by-12 boundary
- Conducts himself improperly or makes serious improper remarks to the referee (A competitor also loses a point if his coach commits this offense.)

WEIGHT CLASSES

Competitors who've not yet earned a black belt generally compete in one of only three weight classes: light, middle, or heavy. Tournament directors determine the weight divisions for these junior and senior men and women. In junior and senior black belt divisions, most state, national, and international contests abide by weight categories sanctioned by the USTU and the WTF. Weight divisions may change on occasion, depending on the number of available competitors. Table 12.1 lists the international weight classifications for men and women. Table 12.2 shows the weight limits for 13- to 16-year-old junior boys and girls.

PREPARING FOR COMPETITION

You can't achieve peak performance in the ring without physical and mental preparation for competition. It's not enough just to know which targets to attack and which kicks to employ. Those

TABLE 12.1
International Weight Classifications

Class	Men	Women
Fin	Not exceeding 110 lbs/ 50 kg	Not exceeding 94.6 lbs/ 43 kg
Fly	Over 110-118.8 lbs/ 50-54 kg	Over 94.6-103.4 lbs/ 43-47 kg
Bantam	Over 118.8-127.6 lbs/ 54-58 kg	Over 103.4-112.2 lbs/ 47-51 kg
Feather	Over 127.6-140.8 lbs/ 58-65 kg	Over 112.2-121.0 lbs/ 51-55 kg
Light	Over 140.8-154.0 lbs/ 65-70 kg	Over 121.0-132.0 lbs/ 55-60 kg
Welter	Over 154.0-167.2 lbs/ 70-76 kg	Over 132.0-143.0 lbs/ 60-65 kg
Middle	Over 167.2-182.6 lbs/ 76-83 kg	Over 143.0-154.0 lbs/ 65-70 kg
Heavy	Over 182.6 lbs/83 kg	Over 154.0 lbs/70 kg

TABLE 12.2
Junior Sparring Weight Classifications for Black Belts Aged 15-18

Class	Male or Female
Super fin	Under 85.9 lbs/39 kg
Fin	86.0-94.9 lbs/39-43 kg
Fly	95.0-103.9 lbs/43-47 kg
Bantam	104.0-114.9 lbs/47-52 kg
Feather	115.0-123.9 lbs/52-56 kg
Light	124.0-132.9 lbs/56-60 kg
Welter	133.0-143.9 lbs/60-65 kg
Middle	144.0-154.9 lbs/65-70 kg
Heavy	155.0-164.9 lbs/70-75 kg
Super heavy	Over 165.0 lbs/75 kg

COMPETITION TERMS

KOREAN	ENGLISH
bae sim	juror
barro	return
bu sim	judge
gam-jeum	point deducted
gu-mahn	end
hwee-jeon	a competition round
jeum	a point scored
joo sim	referee
kae-sok	continue
kalyeo	break
kyong-ye	bow
kyong-go	warning penalty
si-jak	begin
sung	win

flashy technicians who know nothing of mental toughness usually lose in the early rounds of tournaments. You, however, have the opportunity to surpass your previous performance each time you step into the ring. Follow the suggestions in this section and exercise your mental preparation skills daily. Let your mind direct your body to be your best.

You must commit time and physical effort to be able to fight at your best. Don't take competition lightly. Focus your attention on your goal, and exclude all other distractions. The extra sparring, stretching, and bag work is only part of your preparation. You may need to revise your social calendar and modify your diet. *Make a list of everything you should do or not do to reach your goal.*

Develop a training schedule. Begin training for your tournament at least three months in advance. Longer isn't always better, because you might injure yourself or get stale if you focus intensely for more than three months. If you lose in the first round of one tournament, plan to enter a back-up tournament so you can compete again while you are in peak condition. Don't train harder for your back-up tournament; train smarter. Remind yourself to relax and to enjoy.

Surround yourself with motivation. Family and friends can give you a tremendous boost. Training partners who share your hopes and dreams can enrich your growth and strengthen your commitment. Read the latest taekwondo magazines and watch the best action flicks. Display photographs and reminders of your best performances. These mementos transmit a powerful energy of the events they portray. Immerse yourself in your goal to heighten your motivation. If you are tempted to skip a training session, remind yourself that you are a warrior.

Train hard, but don't overtrain. Your body can break down when you overexert. If you listen to your body, it will tell you when to fight hard and when to relax. Using high energy all of the time can be counterproductive. Train hard for short periods. If you cross train, allow extra rest between practice sessions. Never train the same muscle groups intensely two days in a row. Spar at a competitive level no more than twice a week so your body has a chance to repair itself. Use common sense and follow the general guidelines in *Taekwondo Techniques & Tactics*.

Test yourself occasionally. Participate in a mock tournament once a week (but no more than that). Employ judges and time-keepers, and wear all of the gear you normally use in the ring. Pretend the "tournament" is genuine, but keep it fun. Follow a precompetition eating and drinking routine, and get used to crowds and noise. Competing in several of these preliminary tune-up tournaments will prepare you for the real thing.

Choosing a tournament to compete in may be difficult. Survey your rivals to see if you measure up or if you'll have a hard time winning a single bout. If you competed well in a certain tournament, go back. Simple things such as knowing the arena and the hotels can be an advantage when you can't afford to waste nervous energy.

Develop a strategy for each bout. Enter your tournament understanding what you want to do and how you want to do it. Scout your opponents and plan your tactics. Continue using your original game plan unless you are obviously overmatched, but have a back-up strategy. Identify what you must do against your opponents, practice it thoroughly during training, and give yourself some flexibility on tournament day.

Persevere no matter what. You may not win the tournament, or even a single bout, but don't give up. Learn from each experience and you'll soon be winning. Tournaments are games, and the more you play, the better you'll get. Don't make excuses for losing. Instead, evaluate why you lost, accept the reasons, and press forward.

Pack your uniform, protective gear, energy bars, and drinks days before your event. Arrange for your transportation, entrance fees, and hotel. Upon arriving at the tournament site, look over the arena and find the restrooms and warm-up areas. Eat a well-balanced meal at a familiar restaurant on the morning of the tournament. Arrive at the arena several hours before your event is scheduled to begin. Give yourself at least two hours to check in and warm up.

MENTAL TOUGHNESS

Some say competition is an acceptable way to vent aggression. Others believe it exposes strengths and weaknesses in personalities. There is little doubt that the heat of battle exposes a competitor's weakest points. A taekwondoist with a negative personality may turn against himself in the ring as his hidden vulnerabilities become apparent. Competition is connected to his image. A physically strong, athletic competitor who works hard may look great in training, but in the ring he may fade at the first sign of trouble. He loses confidence, his fighting spirit diminishes, and he looks helpless. The composed and rational side of his personality is replaced by rage, aggression, whining, or helplessness.

Your mental toughness largely defines how successful you'll be in the ring. No matter how mentally tough you are or how hard you try, there are probably a few chinks in your competitive armor. These chinks may range from excess anxiety to decreased confidence. Whatever these gaps or breaks are, they invariably block your ability to perform to your potential.

How well taekwondoists control their mind determines why some choke and others remain calm and focused. Overcoming emotional weakness is really the toughest part of training, especially if your defects overwhelm you. Turn your deficiencies into functional outcomes. Start by cataloging your weaknesses. Do you get too nervous? Do you get angry? Establish a code of behavior so your anxiety or fury cannot surface. Then change your anxiety into energy and your anger into competitive zeal. By increasing awareness of your mental strengths and weaknesses, you'll be better equipped to consistently perform toward the upper range of your ability.

PSYCHOLOGY OF COMBAT

Your mental attitude can make the difference between winning or losing an important match. Incorporate the following tips into your mental preparation before a match and use them to bolster your confidence and keep on track while competing.

Make sure your schedule allows you to focus on your upcoming event. Spend at least 15 minutes each day mentally preparing for battle. You have no control over the caliber of your opponent, but you can be sure you fight *your* best. Win the mental battle before setting foot in the ring. See and feel yourself as graceful and powerful, fast and strong, flexible and tenacious, deceptive and direct, cool and spontaneous, invincible, the winner. In your mind, experience yourself overcoming one opponent after another. Get yourself pumped up by imagining that you are fighting for the

world championship. Think about past successes. Remember the exhilaration of winning.

Before and during each bout, get pumped: Be enthusiastic, vigorous, alert, and energetic, but don't forget to relax between rounds. Don't rush when you hear the bell, but act confident and energized. Thrive on having fun in the ring. Maintain a positive attitude throughout each match, and let a supportive crowd spur you to your best performance. If you project a confident image regardless of the score, the momentum will shift your way. Remember that toughness is just as important as talent. Well-schooled competitors with perfect kicks can lose to scrappy fighters. On any given day *anyone* can be beaten.

Be acutely tuned in to yourself during a match. Pay attention to your mental state in various situations. You may notice that your mind wanders at critical times. It's okay to zone out during warm-up, but when the fight begins, focus and clear your mind.

Finally, fight your best without obsessing about the outcome. Don't try too hard. Relax and let your movements flow.

Hyperintensity increases the likelihood that you'll make mistakes. Say key words to yourself such as "relax" and "focus." Smile when you feel anxious. Slow down when you're nervous. Focus on the present.

IMAGERY

Using imagery can improve your performance in self-defense and competition. Many of the athletes on the United States Taekwondo team have found imagery to be very beneficial to their performance. Imagine yourself scoring with a front kick. Can you see it? Can you feel it?

You can use two types of imagery to improve your taekwondo performance: internal and external. The internal type uses your ability to "feel" yourself performing. With external imagery, you imagine yourself punching and kicking as if you were watching yourself on television.

Relaxation is a vital prerequisite to internal imagery, external imagery, and taekwondo performance. Try to be relaxed in any situation. If something bothers you, ask yourself why, then fix it. If you can't fix it, don't let it bother you. Breathe from your diaphragm if something excites you. Take moments during the day to relax. But more than that, weave those precious seconds into the fabric of your entire day. Listen to soothing music, play a board game, enjoy a warm bath. When you do not feel that you have time to relax, this is when you need relaxation the most. You *will* lose your cool now and then, so prepare for it and let it go. When you feel anger, notice it; then give it up. Work on relaxation techniques a little bit each day. Become more relaxed, more focused, more fun.

Using relaxation and imagery may not make you as quick as Bruce Lee, but studies show that 10 minutes of daily training and practice with these techniques can improve your taekwondo performance. Researchers Bob Weinberg, Allen Jackson, and Tom Seabourne demonstrated that a combination of relaxation and imagery benefited taekwondo students more than either relaxation or imagery alone did. Taekwondo students who practiced relaxation and imagery 10 minutes every single day performed significantly better than people who were exposed to the technique just moments before their performance. When taekwondoists individualized imagery to their specific needs, they performed better than a control group did and better than their own previous performances. And you don't need an instructor in order to use imagery effectively. The research showed that instructor-guided imagery was no more effective than self-guided imagery.

Internal Imagery. Recent research suggests that imagery is most effective when practiced from the internal perspective, which is not surprising because internal imagery may enhance innervation of the proper nerve to muscle pathways. When performing the internal imagery technique described in the following list, you may actually feel your muscles twitch as they respond to your mental machinations. Use as many of your senses as possible. Try to "feel" the move as if you were actually performing it. "Hear" the sound of the technique as it snaps through the air. "See" yourself performing the movement, then physically practice the movement by shadow boxing. Practice both physically and mentally until your physical technique approaches the perfection of your mental ideal.

Two-Minute Internal Imagery Technique

1. Close your eyes and relax (10 seconds).
2. Focus on your breath as you breathe from your diaphragm (20 seconds).
3. See, feel, and experience yourself punching, kicking, striking, and blocking (30 seconds).
4. Take another few moments to practice your favorite technique over and over in your mind (30 seconds).
5. Enjoy a sensation of perfect balance, control, and heightened speed and flexibility (10 seconds).
6. Let these feelings reinforce themselves (10 seconds).
7. Slowly open your eyes (10 seconds).

External Imagery. While internal imagery allows you to view your techniques through your eyes only, external imagery gives you the opportunity to visualize your movements as an outsider watching yourself perform. To practice external imagery, make a mental picture of a perfect movement that you have witnessed in a martial arts movie or taekwondo tournament. Review the move over and over in your mind. Now you become the actor. See a vivid and controllable image of yourself performing a perfect punch or kick. *Vividness* refers to the clarity of your mental picture. The nervous system perceives vividly imagined events as actual experiences. If the visual model is unclear, the beneficial feedback to your musculature may not occur. To produce a vivid image, see yourself as if you are part of an audience watching you on screen. Visualize your whole body, including the back of your head. *Controllability* refers to whether the image acts according to your wishes. Imagine yourself throwing perfect punches, kicks, strikes, and blocks with speed, balance, and control. Don't make mistakes in your technique: If you are "seeing" yourself perform an exemplary kick, be careful that your illusory body does not slip and fall. Practice a variety of blocks, kicks, and punches using external imagery to solidify the correct movements in your mind.

Although taekwondo was created as an art for self-defense, there is no denying its appeal as a sport. Under the guidance of the WTF, taekwondo continues to thrive as an international sport. Part of the reason for taekwondo's success is that it is safe, pleasurable, and a useful learning experience. The actual competition in the ring is enticing. The adrenaline rush is incredible. One-on-one, winner takes all. Winning is celebrating; losing is learning. Taekwondo competitors understand that fighting is part of the journey. Competition is a gauge to measure improvement.

CHAPTER

13

CONDITIONING

Elite taekwondo competitors are among the best-conditioned athletes in the world. Most exhibit impressive strength and sport well-defined muscles. They possess incredible staying power, not to mention tight waistlines. And taekwondoists can stretch into awesome positions.

Whether you compete in the ring or are attacked in the street, you will be a better fighter if you have flexibility, strength, power, resilience, speed, agility, and stamina. You may have been born with some of these traits, but you'll have to develop others through a solid conditioning program. This chapter gives you some basic guidelines and exercises to help you develop one.

You know your weaknesses. Use the cardiovascular, flexibility, plyometric, abdominal, resistance, punching bag and target pad, and breathing exercises in this section to train until you overcome your weaknesses. Time and again, the talented are beaten by those who have trained and pushed harder.

CARDIOVASCULAR TRAINING

Cardiovascular training gives you the endurance to complete three, three-minute rounds of full-contact taekwondo without huffing and puffing. Taekwondo training in the dojang gives you an excellent aerobic workout. Punching, kicking, blocking, and stepping have all of the ingredients for cardiovascular success. More important, you'll use these techniques during competition or combat. Punching and kicking are the best ways to improve your endurance for punching and kicking. Cross training (training with different activities like running, swimming, etc.) can help, but the more closely your cardiovascular practice resembles your taekwondo activity, the better.

Jumping Rope

Jumping rope is a superb warm-up exercise and cardiovascular activity. It's an inexpensive way to improve your footwork and prepare for taekwondo training. Choose a plastic jump rope, because cotton ropes swing slow and leather ropes wear out. To measure your rope, stand on the middle of the rope and hold one end in each hand. Both ends should reach your armpits.

Turn the rope with your wrists. Hold your hands at your waist about two inches from your body and spin the rope so it barely touches the floor. Jump low, and land lightly on the balls of your feet, knees bent, to take the strain off your shins. Jump rope on wood floors, rubber floors, or rubber tiles to avoid stressing your joints. Jump three, one-minute rounds with a 30-second rest between each round. Vary the intensity by altering the types and number of jumps you do. You can skip, do double hops, or cross your arms to keep practice interesting while building cardio-vascular endurance and muscular strength and endurance in your calves. Increase your duration one minute per round each week until you can jump three, three-minute rounds. Jump rope every other day.

Flexibility

Stretching is used to enhance your range of motion and prevent injuries. After you have warmed your muscles by jumping rope or jogging in place it's time to stretch. (For safety, never stretch a cold muscle.) A full-body stretching program takes no more than 10 minutes to finish. Those who stretch every day can maintain a high degree of flexibility. Sixty-year-old Korean master Tiger Kim can jump up, break a board, and then land gracefully in a full split.

Many factors affect flexibility. On warm days, you can touch your toes; on cooler days, you barely reach your knees. You can hold your stretch more comfortably in the afternoon than in the morning. Perform your routine with the grace and control of Olympic taekwondo champion Herb Perez limbering up for a fight scene.

STRETCHING TECHNIQUES

Thirty years ago, exercisers bounced through their stretches. However, researchers discovered that bounce (ballistic) stretching can cause microtears in the muscles. Twenty years ago, instructors emphasized slow and gentle stretching. Another decade passed, and proprioceptive neuromuscular facilitation (PNF) came into vogue. PNF, a technique where you flex a muscle moments before you stretch it, continues to be widely used today to stretch every skeletal muscle in the body. A new program, called active-isolated (AI) stretching, is also fashionable. AI stretching dictates that you flex the opposing muscle group moments before you stretch. For example, to loosen up your lower back, flex your abdominal muscles first; then hold your back stretch for two seconds. To stretch your calf muscles, flex the muscles on your shins moments prior to stretching your calves. Both PNF and AI allow the muscle and connective tissue to relax and lengthen. To begin your personalized taekwondo stretching program, choose some of the individual and partner stretches in the following sections. Do just one repetition of each stretch.

INDIVIDUAL STRETCHES

Perform the following exercises as AI stretches by flexing the opposite muscle group moments before holding the suggested stretch for 10 to 30 seconds. In the side leg stretch, flex your outer thigh by isometrically contracting your quadriceps muscle. Hold for three seconds, then relax. Stretch your inner thigh by performing a slow, continuous lengthening of the muscle during the stretching phase. Elongate your muscle until you feel tension, then relax. Go for comfort. Settle into your pose. Exhale as you move into each position. Learn to hold your stretch at least 10 seconds to fully relax the muscle. Add 2 seconds a week until you work up to 30 seconds. Within a few months of beginning your stretching program, you may feel a slight level of discomfort during a stretch, but the feeling should never approach pain.

SIDE LEG

Your supporting foot remains flat while you extend your other leg to the side. Flex your outer thigh for three seconds. Relax, then stretch your inner thigh until it feels taut. Hold the stretch for no longer than 30 seconds. Repeat with the other leg.

SIDE SPLIT

Spread your legs out as far as possible. Flex your hips and thighs for three seconds. Relax. Let your weight nudge you down until you feel pressure in your inner thighs. Hold the stretch for up to 30 seconds.

SIDE SPLIT WITH TOES UP, CHEST TO FLOOR

Attempt a side split, then lift your toes. Flex your thighs and hips for three seconds. Relax. Slowly bring your chest toward the floor. When you feel tension, hold for up to 30 seconds.

FRONT SPLIT

Sit on the floor with one leg extended out in front of you and one stretched out behind you. Flex your front thigh and the muscles in the front of your shin by pulling your toes back for three seconds. Relax, then point your toes and pull your chest toward your knee and your forehead toward your shin. Maintain a flat back. When you feel light pressure, hold for up to 30 seconds. Repeat with the other leg.

FOREHEAD TO TOES

Sit with your back flat and the bottoms of your feet together. Pull your feet in as close to your groin as possible and grab your toes. Flex your inner thighs for three seconds. Relax, and slowly bring your chest toward your toes. Hold for up to 30 seconds.

BUTTERFLY

From the forehead to toes position, grab your feet and push your knees toward the floor with your elbows. Hold for up to 30 seconds.

PARTNER STRETCHES

PNF stretching with a partner can help you achieve optimum flexibility. Relax the muscle you intend to stretch as your partner pulls you slowly toward a perfect pose. When you feel tension in the target muscle, instruct your partner to stop. Flex that muscle for three seconds against your partner's resistance. Then your partner attempts to pull just a little farther. She draws you once again to the point of tension, holds, and then allows you to relax. Push and pull gently when your partner is doing the stretches.

HAMSTRING

Lie on your back with your heels flat against the floor and both knees slightly bent. Press the back of your heels into the floor and hold for three seconds. Relax. Let your partner grab your right ankle and slowly lift it. When you feel tension, instruct your partner to stop. Pull from your right hamstring and press the back of your heel toward the floor while your partner resists for three seconds. Relax, and repeat with your left leg.

HIP

Lie on your stomach with your knees slightly bent. Flex the front of your thighs by pressing them toward the floor. Hold for three seconds. Relax. Let your partner grab your right ankle and slowly lift it until you feel tension. Be sure the toes on your right foot point down. When you feel tension, remind your partner to stop. For three seconds, pull from your hip toward the floor  while your partner resists. Relax and repeat with your left leg.

INNER THIGH

 Sit facing a partner. Both of you spread your legs as far as possible in a straddle position. Flex your thighs and hips for three seconds. Relax. Place your feet against your partner's and push lightly until both of you feel a maximum stretch. Hold for up to 30 seconds.

Plyometrics

The United States Olympic Taekwondo team uses plyometric training to boost the power of their punches and kicks, and so can you. The objective in taekwondo is to generate the greatest amount of force in the shortest period of time. When you break a board, it's not just how hard you hit it, but how fast. Plyometrics combines speed and strength to improve explosiveness. Training for power includes both strength training and speed work. Power is speed applied to strength. It's important to be strong, but the taekwondoist who applies strength and speed effectively is the one who will hit the hardest. Plyometrics also helps you move and change directions faster.

Plyometrics consists of a variety of drills that train your nervous system and metabolic pathways to increase your strength and power. Plyometric bounding takes advantage of the muscles' stretch-recoil and stretch-reflex properties. Researchers believe that the brief stretch you feel in your muscle during push-off increases muscle contraction, enhancing explosiveness. During plyometric exercises, the central nervous system brings about involuntary neuromuscular contraction. Plyometric training requires you to accelerate through a complete range of motion and then to relax into a full stretch. It gives the sensation of sequentially contracting all of your muscles, leading to maximum explosive power in your attacks and increased impact of your techniques. Use this very vigorous form of exercise only twice a week, preferably following your taekwondo training. After a few months of plyometrics, kicking will seem easier. Not only will you get stronger, you will be able to train harder and longer. Your body will not succumb as easily to the lactic acid burn during intense training. Your heart will pump blood and oxygen more efficiently to your muscles, so your anaerobic threshold will increase.

Before beginning plyometric training, be sure to jog or jump rope for five minutes and then stretch. Take it easy on your first few sets and repetitions of plyometrics. Spend at least 30 seconds resting between sets, but perform each repetition one right after the other. After a month of plyometrics, you may spend less time between sets and increase to two sets of 20 repetitions.

PLYOMETRICS FOR PUNCHING POWER

A faster punch is more powerful, and plyometric exercises for the upper body increase the speed, strength, and explosiveness of your punches. They increase strength in your shoulders, triceps, chest, and back, which translates into increased force in all of your upper-body movements. Begin with five repetitions. Add one repetition each week until you can perform 20 repetitions.

CLAP PUSH-UPS

From a push-up position, extend your arms so your hands leave the floor. Clap your hands before they return to the floor.

DOUBLE CLAP PUSH-UPS

Do a Clap Push-Up, but clap your hands twice before they return to the floor.

LATERAL PUSH-UPS

Start in a push-up position. As you extend your arms forcefully so that your hands leave the floor, shift both hands six inches to your left before returning them to the floor. On your next push-up, shift your hands back to where they began. Follow this by shifting your hands six inches to the right and then back to the center again.

WALL-UPS

With your hands a little less then shoulder width apart, perform a handstand using a wall for balance. Bend your elbows slightly and push back up into a handstand.

PLYOMETRICS FOR KICKING POWER

Plyometric training is an excellent method for improving your kicks. Your leg and hip strength will improve, increasing the speed and explosiveness of all your kicks. The only requirement for plyometric kicking is a wooden or padded floor or a soft backyard. When you begin plyometric training, jump no more than two inches off the ground. Add one inch each week until you are jumping as high as you can.

FRONT STANCE JUMPS

Begin in a front stance. Jump up 10 times and switch in the air to a back stance so each foot replaces the other. Take no rest between jumps.

JUMP FRONT KICK, ALTERNATE

Raise your right knee forcefully to come off the floor. Let your left leg follow your right leg as you are airborne, and throw a front kick. Fall softly to the floor, rolling from the balls of your feet to your heels. Repeat with your left leg. Perform 10 consecutive jumps, alternating kicks each jump.

PREPARE TO FLIP

Jump up, bringing your knees up to your chest. Try to keep your feet together and tuck your hands around your knees. Do 10 repetitions.

AWAKEN THE LION

From a relaxed position with your fingers touching the floor, bound up as high as you can. Land in the same position in which you began. Do 10 repetitions.

KNEE STRIKES

Stand in a front stance and drive your back knee up fast and hard, pulling your front foot slightly off the floor. Pull your hands down on each strike. Extend the other leg back and alternate knees. Do 10 repetitions.

ABDOMINAL EXERCISES

The most vital area to tone and strengthen is your torso. Strong abdominal muscles stabilize the spine, protect you from injury, and help you endure blows. Abdominal muscles allow your torso to twist and bend so you can block, punch, and strike. The abdominal muscles connect your upper body to your lower body at your waist, and the waist's twisting generates the tremendous torque necessary for dynamic kicks. Strong stomach muscles also enhance your balance and protect your internal organs.

Imagine yourself with rock-hard abdominal muscles. Visualize a suit of muscular armor around your torso. This solid band of muscle generates speed and strength, providing superior power in your punches, kicks, jumps, twists, and throws.

The muscles in the front and side of the belly help your legs raise to throw powerful, thrusting kicks. The muscles that run diagonally across the ribs and those that sit above them help you withstand a blow. Curl up slowly on all abdominal exercises. "Feel" the muscles working. Place your hands under your hips if you have a delicate back. Begin with 10 repetitions. Add two each week until you can complete 50 repetitions without resting. Practice the following exercises every other day, including the bodywork segment with a partner, to ensure your progress.

CRUNCHES

Lie on your back with your knees bent and your chin resting on your chest. Curl your head and shoulders upward and forward off the floor until the small of your back begins to leave the floor. Hold for three seconds, then flex your abdominal muscles on the way down. The range of motion is only a few inches, so don't raise your torso as you would in a regular sit-up. Do 10 repetitions. Add two repetitions a week until you can complete 50 crunches.

REVERSE CRUNCHES

Lie on your back with your knees bent, feet flat on the floor, and hands under your hips. Squeeze your knees together as you bring them to your chest. Hold for three seconds, then let your feet slowly descend to the floor. Contract your lower abdominals. Do 10 repetitions. Add two repetitions a week until you can finish 50.

OBLIQUE TWISTS

Lie on your back with your arms out to each side, perpendicular to your body. Raise your legs, with your knees slightly bent, to create a 90-degree angle between your stomach and your thighs. Bring your legs down to your right side so your knees barely touch the floor. Repeat, bringing your legs across your midline down to your left side. Alternate sides, doing 10 repetitions each. Add two repetitions a week until you can perform 25 repetitions on each side.

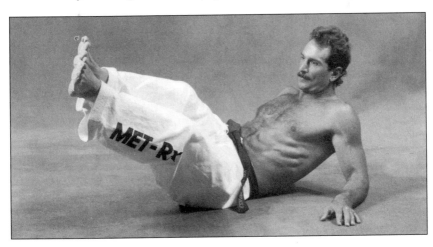

BODY WORK

After you've done the crunches and reverse crunches, let your partner lightly punch your front and side abdominals. With each punch, exhale just before your partner contacts. Flex the section about to be hit. Body work requires your partner to make light contact to all areas of your upper torso so you develop confidence to withstand an assault.

RESISTANCE TRAINING

The stronger you are, the better you'll be at taekwondo. The goal of working out with weights is to increase muscular endurance and strength, confidence, and fighting ability. Resistance training is a superb form of exercise, strengthening cartilage and muscle tissue. Added strength aids your ability to absorb a punch as well as to throw a powerful one. Muscles help you keep your balance, recover if you fall, and strike faster and harder. Men and women taekwondoists who train with weights generally have more flexibility and endurance and a leaner body than nonlifters.

Through the years, elite taekwondoists have become increasingly powerful. They know that strength training prevents injuries and improves performance. Balance your approach to resistance training. If you use them properly, weights do not slow you or hamper your endurance. Perform the lifts prior to taekwondo training, when your muscles have usable stores of energy. Use free weights, when you can, rather than machines, because they allow you to move in specific punching and blocking patterns. Train with resistance equipment two to four times a week for an hour.

Train each muscle group twice a week. Ease into your workout. Select a weight you can comfortably control. Begin with easy repetitions, then gradually increase the intensity. Breathe normally during an exercise. If you are exerting, however, exhale during the contraction. Inhale on the short rests between each contraction. Hold your stomach in, relax your neck, keep your back flat (don't arch). Focus on the specific muscle group you are training. Feel the muscle work in each repetition. The amount of weight you lift should never compromise your form. Explode into your movement with a controlled, 100-percent, energized effort. Imagine a surge of power as the blood enters the working muscle. Move the weight through a full range of motion. Stretch each muscle group following each set.

The key to improving your strength and muscular endurance is training smart. Begin with push-ups and crunches. In a few months, work your way up to using dumbbells and ankle weights. Resistance training will strengthen your entire body. A full-body workout on Mondays and Thursdays allows you enough recuperation to make colossal gains.

STRIKE AND BLOCK RESISTANCE TRAINING

To develop muscular strength and endurance in the arms and shoulders, practice blocking and punching with hand weights. The following is a list of just some of the blocks and strikes you can perform:

- Double rising block. Then singles.
- Double middle block. Then singles.
- Double downward block. Then singles.
- Middle downward block. Then singles.
- Double front punch. Then singles.
- Right reverse punch. Then switch hands.

- Double back fist strike. Then singles.
- Rising block, reverse punch. Then switch hands.
- Middle block, reverse punch. Then switch hands.
- Downward block, reverse punch. Then switch hands.
- Triple punch (high, middle, low). Then switch hands.

Make sure your posture is perfect. Maintain compact form and slow down all your movements so you never hyperextend your elbows or shoulders. Perform 10 repetitions of each hand technique with a weight light enough to maintain perfect form. Practice at about one-fifth of your normal speed, and expect a slight burning sensation in the muscles you are working. Add one repetition to each exercise per week until you can do 20 repetitions of each exercise with perfect form. When you can perform 20 repetitions, gradually increase the weight of your dumbbells and go back to doing only 10 repetitions. Continue the cycle of increased repetitions and increased weight. Your muscles will adapt to heavier weight over time. As you increase the weight, you will gain strength. Be patient. Do not train a muscle if it is sore from a previous workout. If you feel joint pain, lighten the resistance (weight). At the conclusion of your weighted hands routine, throw some fast, hard blocks and punches without dumbbells to amplify your speed and power.

KICK RESISTANCE TRAINING

Throwing double and triple kicks was Tom Seabourne's taekwondo tournament specialty. He didn't have a natural ability to hold his leg up; he trained two days a week with ankle weights.

To improve leg strength in your double and triple kicks, strap three-pound ankle weights to each leg. Hold a wall or chair for balance and cock your leg high with your heel close to your hip and the side of your knee parallel to the floor in a roundhouse kick position. Extend your leg slowly without dropping the knee. Do 10 repetitions with each leg. Perform the same program with a side kick, side hook kick, front kick, and back kick. Rest 30 seconds between sets. Add one repetition per week on all of your kicks until you can perform 20 repetitions with each different kick. After you can do 20 repetitions, use five-pound ankle weights and do 10 repetitions with each kick. Continue the series of increased repetitions until you can perform 20 repetitions with perfect form for every kick. Never increase your ankle weights more than five pounds at a time. After completing your repetitions, remove your ankle weights, face a mirror in a sparring position, and bounce lightly on the balls of your feet. Practice all of your kicks, especially

double kicks, and mix them up, using several different angles of attack. Kick for five minutes. Afterward, spend a few minutes cooling down with your stretching routine.

PUNCHING BAG AND TARGET PAD TRAINING

In the first few months of taekwondo training, your instructor will teach you perfect form for punches and kicks. For those months, your training aid is a mirror. As you progress, you may wonder if your punches and kicks are effective. At that point, your instructor may introduce you to a punching bag and target pad. Bag work and target pad training will increase your speed, power, and agility. Your performance depends largely on the intensity of your training, and these methods will give you the chance to go all out without injuring a sparring partner.

BAG WORK

If you train alone, a punching bag is a solid substitute for a good partner. Be sure to use the following tips before starting your bag work.

Always warm up before striking the bag, then begin slowly. Relax and focus. Maintain proper form. Launch your movement with a twist of your hips for each punch or kick. When you punch, use bag gloves. Make sure that you hit the bag with your first two knuckles. When you kick, make contact with the top, ball, heel, or side of your foot. Perform single techniques first (e.g., jab, reverse punch, hook, front kick, roundhouse kick, side kick, back kick, and so on), then perform your combinations exactly as you would use them in sparring When practicing combinations, keep your hands up, stay light on your feet, and imagine the bag as your opponent. Cool down by "free sparring" with the bag, and gradually slow your pace. Conclude with stretching.

TARGET PAD TRAINING

Your partner can help you sharpen your kicks, punches, and strikes with foam rubber target pads. Warm up and stretch before you begin. Kick or punch slowly at first. Touch the pad with each kick or strike. After a thorough warm-up, snap your kicks and strikes through the pad with speed. Hit fast, and retract your foot or arm quickly, like you're cracking a whip with each hit. Hit with the appropriate part of your foot or hand. The reverberating "thwack" you hear when your foot or hand hits the pad highlights the speed and power of the strike. Allow your partner to hold a pad

in each hand to give you moving targets. Each time he angles the target, execute a different kick or strike. For example, if the target is facing down, do a front kick. If it is at a 45-degree angle, throw a roundhouse kick. If it is perpendicular to the floor, shoot a side kick. Throw your kicks and strikes from the same posture you use in a fight or during competition. Focus on your partner's solar plexus and see the pads with your peripheral vision.

FOCUSED BREATHING

The last detail a taekwondoist considers is breathing. (That is, until he is gasping after throwing one kick too many!) Breathing techniques can help you to relax and add power to your punches and kicks. Proper breathing also enables you to withstand a blow to your midsection. Simple breathing exercises practiced in or out of the dojang can help you build that profound connection between your mind and body.

It is important to breathe through your nose during taekwondo training to decrease anxiety and stay focused. Nose breathing prevents you from gulping air, so you pace yourself. Breathe deeply through your nose during competition or combat. Make each breath long, deep, and slow, allowing your body to remain relaxed even under extreme stress.

Infants breathe through their noses from their diaphragms. When they cry, they breathe through their mouths, huffing and puffing from their upper chests. Scared rabbits and nervous taekwondoists do the same. Most novice taekwondoists breathe through their mouths and rarely use their full lung capacity. Some don't breathe at all when they throw punches and kicks, which creates unnecessary tension. Because they were not taught about breathing, they use a small percentage of their lung capacity.

To learn to breathe from your diaphragm instead of from your chest, lie on your back, place your left hand on your chest, and rest your right hand on your stomach. Inhale deeply through your nose for five seconds, focusing on raising your diaphragm. Let the air fill your chest cavity, starting low and expanding up. Then take about seven seconds to exhale slowly through your mouth by lowering your diaphragm. Only your right hand should move as you breathe deeply from your abdomen. Diaphragmatic breathing

RELAXATION EXERCISE

Sit with your back straight and take a deep breath from your diaphragm until your stomach puffs out. Exhale and allow tension in any part of your body to be released. Focus only on your breathing. Let nothing distract or disturb you; just breathe. If thoughts or sounds interfere, ignore them. Close this book, close your eyes, and continue your relaxation. After five minutes, slowly come out of your relaxed state. How do you feel? Close your eyes and continue your relaxation for 20 minutes. Warning: Do not lie down unless your goal is to sleep!

allows you to get more oxygen to your working muscles. Notice how muscles in your body spontaneously relax.

Train your lungs the same way you train your body for punches and kicks. Take a deep breath and hold it. Stretch your lungs to their limit. Lungs may lose flexibility the way an unstretched muscle does. To relax, breathe in deeply through your nose to fill your lungs. If you get rattled during a confrontation, concentrate on your deep-breathing inhalation-exhalation cycle to eliminate other stimuli. Your ribs will feel as if they are squeezing an overfilled balloon when you don't breath regularly and deeply from your diaphragm. Focused breathing builds lung capacity, eases stress, energizes you, and prepares your body and mind for taekwondo.

Use focused breathing to increase your energy. Exhale each time you throw a punch or kick. Exhaling forcefully increases the power in your technique. A ki-hop adds a vocalization to your exhalation. Not only will this shout from your diaphragm add strength to your attack, but it may also demoralize your opponent.

As a beginner, your training in the dojang may be uncomfortable. You will move your body in ways it has never moved before. Your taekwondo training time is restricted, and you may lack the ability to throw powerful techniques. Whether you are confronted in self-defense or competing in sparring or poomse, you may fade. Several months into your training, your body will adapt to arduous work. Your strength, endurance, and flexibility will increase.

An additional plyometric, strength, and flexibility program will further your progress. Be sure to schedule these supplemental workouts when they will not interfere with your dojang training. You will be a better fighter if you can enhance your speed, endurance, flexibility, and strength. You can always improve your physical condition, and doing so will benefit you in many ways. You'll have more energy, strength, and endurance; the quality of your life will be enhanced; and you will sleep better and perform longer.

SUGGESTED READINGS

Benson, H. 1984. *Beyond the relaxation response.* New York: Times Books.

Benson, H. 1987. *Your maximum mind.* New York: Times Books.

Benson, H. 1993. *The wellness book.* New York: Simon & Schuster.

Borysenko, J. 1988. *Minding the body, mending the mind.* New York: Bantam.

Csikszentmihalyi, M. 1994. *Flow: The psychology of optimal experience.* New York: Simon & Schuster.

Dossey, L. 1993. *Healing words.* New York: Harper Collins.

Freidman, M. 1989. A master of moving meditation. *New Realities,* June, 11-20.

Goleman, D. 1993. *Mind body medicine.* Yonkers, NY: Consumer Reports Books.

Langer, E. 1989. *Mindfulness.* New York: Addison Wesley.

Loehr, J. 1995. Mentally tough. *Tennis,* December, 28-29.

Seabourne, T.G. 1986. Cross-court training. *Tae Kwon Do Times,* November, 68, 69.

Seabourne, T.G. 1986. Mental kicks. *Superfit,* Fall, 6.

Seabourne, T.G. 1996. *Cross-training.* Dubuque, IA: Eddie Bowers.

Seabourne, T.G., and E. Herndon. 1986. *Self defense: A body-mind approach.* Scottsdale, AZ: Gorsuch-Scarisbrick.

Seabourne, T.G., and R.S. Weinberg. 1985. Martial mind games: Can you psyche yourself into winning? *Inside Karate,* March, 49-53.

Seabourne, T.G., R.S. Weinberg, and A. Jackson. 1981. Effects of visuo-motor behavior rehearsal, relaxation and imagery on karate performance. *Journal of Sport Psychology* 3 (3): 228-238.

Seabourne, T.G., R.S. Weinberg, and A. Jackson. 1983. Effect of individualized practice and training of visuo-motor behavior rehearsal in enhancing karate performance. *Journal of Sport Behavior* 6: 58-67.

Seabourne, T.G., R.S. Weinberg, and A. Jackson. 1985. Effect of arousal and relaxation instructions prior to the use of imagery. *Journal of Sport Behavior 6:* 209-219.

Seabourne, T.G., R.S. Weinberg, A. Jackson, and R. Suinn. 1985. Effect of individualized, nonindividualized, and packaged cognitive intervention strategies on karate performance. *Journal of Sport Psychology* 7 (1): 40-50.

United States Taekwondo Union Fact Book. 1993. Colorado Springs: United States Taekwondo Union.

Weinberg, R.S., T.G. Seabourne, and A. Jackson. 1982. Effects of visuomotor behavior rehearsal on state-trait anxiety and performance: Is practice important? *Journal of Sport Behavior* 5 (4): 209-218.

Wilmore, J., and D. Costill. 1994. *Physiology of sport and exercise.* Champaign, IL: Human Kinetics.

INDEX

A

Abdominal exercises, 163-166
Amateur Athletic Union (AAU), 14
American Taekwondo Association (ATA), 3
Arm strikes. *See* Punches; Strikes
Attention stance (cha-ryot sogi), 18, 36
Axe kick (nerya cha-gi)
    basic technique, 74-75
    counterattacks to, 126-127

B

Back fist strike (dung-joomock chi-gi), 60-61
Back kick (dwi cha-gi)
    basic technique, 72-73
    as counterattack, 130-131
    spinning, 72, 130-131
Back stance (dwi-gubi sogi), 39
Backward roll (hoo bang nak buhp), 32-33
Backward step, 100
Belts (di), 7-9, 19
Benefits of taekwondo, vii, 2
Blocks (maggi),
    basic guidelines, 21, 83-84
    conditioning for, 167-169
    self-defense tips, 96
    specific blocks, 84-95
        knife hand block, 86-87
        low block, 92-93
        middle inner block, 90-91
        middle outer block, 84-85
        rising block, 88-89
        X-block, 94-95
    terminology, 21
Board breaking (kyukpah), 21, 62-63
Bodhidharma, 11-12
Bowing (kyong-ye), 21
Breakfalling techniques, 26-31. *See also* Falling (nak buhp)
Breaking boards (kyukpah), 21, 62-63
Breathing
    for poomse (forms), 105
    for relaxation, 148, 173
    for taekwondo moves, 172-173

C

Cardiovascular training, 106, 151-152
Children
    belts and ranks, 7-8
    benefits of taekwondo for, vii, 2
    falling skills, 25
    weight categories for competition, 143
Combinations
    basic guidelines, 114-115
    for competition, 120, 122, 124
    crescent kick, double punch, 120-121
    front kick, jab, 116-117
    jab, punch, crescent kick, 122-123
    jab, punch, roundhouse kick, 118-119
    punch, punch, kick, punch, 124-125
    self-defense tips, 122, 124, 135
Competition, 21
    combinations and counterattacks for, 120, 122, 124, 126
    international events, 14
    kicks for, 67-82, 139, 141
    poomse (forms), 106-107
    preparing for, 142, 144-145
    prohibited moves, 52, 54, 56, 60, 140, 141
    psychology of, 145-150
    respect for flags shown at, 19-20
    rules, 9, 137-139
    scoring, 58, 72, 139-140, 141
    stances for, 38
    strikes and punches for, 52-61, 139, 140, 141
    tactics for, 112, 126, 145
    terminology, 143
    weight classes, 140, 142-143
Conditioning
    abdominal exercises, 163-166
    cardiovascular training, 106, 151-152
    flexibility training, 152-158
    plyometrics, 159-163
    punching bag training, 170-171
    resistance training, 166-170
    target pad training, 170, 171-172
Counterattacks
    to axe kick, 126-127

About the Authors

Master Yeon Hwan Park is an eighth-Dan black belt in taekwondo. He runs seven taekwondo schools on Long Island, New York, and serves as the secretary-general of the United States Taekwondo Union (USTU). Park's extensive experience and accomplishments include more than 30 years of competition, teaching, coaching, and developing instructional materials for taekwondo.

Park

Master Park coached the 1988 U.S. Olympic team and the 1991 Pan-American Games team. Since 1984 he has also been the coach of the U.S. National team. Park created a series of six videotapes and has written four other books on taekwondo. Besides his dedication to taekwondo, he enjoys golf and swimming. Park lives in East Meadow, New York, with his wife Kanie, their daughter Nina, and sons Edward and Elliot.

In writing this book, Park was assisted by Peter Zirogiannis, a freelance writer and 1992 silver medalist in the New York State Taekwondo Championships. Zirogiannis is a longtime student and assistant instructor for Master Park. His wife, Marianne, is a black belt, a former gold medalist in the New York State Taekwondo Championships, and a student of Master Park.

Tom Seabourne, PhD, is a sport psychologist and director of physical education at Northeast Texas Community College. He has authored hundreds of articles and three other martial arts and fitness books. A third-Dan black belt in taekwondo and Shorinryu karate, Seabourne is a two-time Amateur Athletic Union and Pan-American Games taekwondo champion and a silver medalist in the World Taekwondo Championships. He is a two-time member of the U.S. National taekwondo team.

Seabourne

Seabourne is a member of the USTU and serves on its medical board. He frequently presents programs to clubs, schools, and industry on achieving peak performance. A world-class cyclist who holds four world ultra-distance cycling records, Seabourne has completed the Race Across America. He lives in Mt. Pleasant, Texas, with his wife Danese, their daughters Alaina, Laura, Julia, and Susanna, and son Grant.